HOW DRUGS CAN AFFECT YOUR LIFE

HOW DRUGS CAN AFFECT YOUR LIFE

The Effects of Drugs on Safety and Well-Being — With Special Emphasis On Prevention of Drug Use

By

WILLIAM A. ALLEN, M.P.H.

NICHOLAS L. PICCONE, Ed.D.

and

CHRISTOPHER D'AMANDA, M.D.

CHARLES C THOMAS • PUBLISHER

Springfield • Illinois • U.S.A.

Published and Distributed Throughout the World by

CHARLES C THOMAS • PUBLISHER
2600 South First Street
Springfield, Illinois, 62717, U.S.A.

ISBN 0-398-04810-X

Library of Congress Catalog Card Number: 82-19558

With THOMAS BOOKS *careful attention is given to all details of manufacturing and design. It is the Publisher's desire to present books that are satisfactory as to their physical qualities and artistic possibilities and appropriate for their particular use.* THOMAS BOOKS *will be true to those laws of quality that assure a good name and good will.*

Printed in the United States of America

I-R-1

Library of Congress Cataloging in Publication Data

Allen, William Austin, 1916-
How drugs can affect your life.

Bibliography: p.
Includes index.
1. Drug abuse. 2. Psychotropic drugs – Physiological effect. 3. Drug abuse – Prevention. I. Piccone, Nicholas L. II. D'Amanda, Christopher. III. Title. [DNLM: 1. Substance abuse – Prevention and control. 2. Substance dependence – Prevention and control. 3. Drugs – Adverse effects. 4. Alcohol, Ethyl – Adverse effects. 5. Smoking – Prevention and control. WM 270 A432h]
RC564.A46 613.8'3 1983 82-19558
ISBN 0-398-04810-X

ABOUT THE AUTHORS

William A. Allen, M.P.H., is a graduate of the University of Minnesota with a master's degree in public health. He served for several years as health educator for the Minnesota Department of Health and is a past president of the Pennsylvania Public Health Association. He is currently Information and Education Officer for the Philadelphia Health Department's Coordinating Office for Drug and Alcohol Abuse Programs. For several years, he served on the faculty of Temple University where he taught courses in community health and school health. He has also lectured at a number of universities and colleges including the University of Minnesota, the University of Pennsylvania, Rutgers University, and Philadelphia Community College. He is co-author of two books, *Learning to Live Without Cigarettes* and *Sex Education for Physically Handicapped Youth.* He served as general secretary of the 1969 Annual Meeting of the American Public Health Association held in Philadelphia. In 1982 he was co-chairman of the Tri-State Health Conference involving Pennsylvania, New Jersey, and Delaware, also conducted in Philadelphia.

Nicholas L. Piccone, Ed.D., served as Director of the Alcohol Highway Safety Program from 1972 to 1979. This innovative program played an important role in reducing fatal accidents in the streets of Philadelphia and was a model for the State of Pennsylvania's "Driving Under the Influence Control System." Before heading the Alcohol Highway Safety Program, Dr. Piccone was a member of the staff of the Managing Director of Philadelphia. From 1963 to 1971, he taught in the city's public school system. His organizational memberships have included the Citizens Advisory Committee to the Governor's Safety Commission, the Steering Committee of the Pennsylvania Driving Under the Influence Association, and the Executive Board of the Philadelphia Forum of Drug and Alcohol Program Directors. Presently, he is Executive Director of the Coordinating Office for Drug and Alcohol Abuse Programs of Philadelphia, a position he has held for the last five years. Dr. Piccone, whose doctoral dissertation provided the first computerized diagnostic scale for objective adjudication of persons arrested for driving under the influence (DUI), has published several papers on the subject.

Christopher D'Amanda, M.D., has seen service in the health field in far-flung regions of the world. From 1966 to 1969, he served in the U.S. Public Health Service assigned as Medical Officer to Ouagadougou, Upper Volta and Abidjan, Ivory Coast, where he took part in the smallpox eradication and measles control program. Among other positions he has held are Director, Erie County Narcotics Registry and Assistant Clinical Professor of Medicine and Psychiatry, Edward J. Meyers Hospital, Buffalo. He is author of a number of articles on drug abuse with particular focus on heroin addiction. Dr. D'Amanda is a member of the Philadelphia County Medical Society and the Pennsylvania State Medical Society, among other groups. He is presently a member of the National Community Correspondents Group, which tracks trends in drug use throughout the nation. A graduate of the School of Medicine, State University of New York at Buffalo, Dr. D'Amanda's current position is Director, Medical Addiction Services, Coordinating Office for Drug and Alcohol Abuse Programs of Philadelphia.

FOREWORD

OF serious concern to Americans of all ages are drug abuse, drug misuse, and drug addiction. Today, these drug problems are found in every part of our society – affluent suburbs, middle class neighborhoods, and slums, whether in the inner city or in small towns. Drug abuse is growing more common on playgrounds, on street corners, in bars, pool halls, and other hangouts, in schools and colleges as well as in business and industry. It is a special problem among teenagers and young adults.

Alcoholism and drug abuse kill 100,000 Americans each year. These diseases touch 75 million Americans annually – more than one in four – and each year cost industry almost sixty-five billion dollars in accidents, production slowdowns, and sickness. Alcoholism and drug abuse lead to half of all arrests in America and cause more than 50 percent of the nation's fatal motor vehicle accidents. Alcoholism and dependency on drug result, not due to a simple lack of willpower, but because they represent diseases, and these diseases cause sadness and grief, not among a few, but among millions.

Drug laws are designed to help control the drug problem, but legislation cannot eliminate it or prevent it. More important in the control of drugs is education, which can furnish youths, their parents, teachers, and counselors with information about the tragic effects on mind and body that often accompany drug abuse and addiction. By making it clear that there are many alternatives to drug use and abuse, education can point the way toward prevention.

There are many reasons why people use drugs. There are more and better reasons why people should not use them. This book is written to assist youths and their parents and teachers in marshalling and using these compelling reasons when dealing with the issue of drug use and abuse.

Some youths are not interested in drugs and do not want to experiment with them. These youths will probably not get into drugs. Other youths have a mild interest in drugs but will probably not become involved with them unless they receive strong pressure from their peers to use them. Still other youths have a definite interest in drugs and do not need much arguing to commence using them. The latter group is "on the fence" regarding drugs and the kind of friends they choose and the crowd they finally decide to go with will often determine whether they will become drug abusers and perhaps even drug addicts.

It should be kept in mind, however, that a youth who never experiments with a drug such as marijuana may end up with early family and work difficulties because of alcohol abuse. Contributing to this possibility are the facts that some 3 million tenth to twelfth graders have alcohol problems, that one in four youths in those grades drink at least once a week, that more high school students use alcohol than any other drug, and that on some college and university campuses, nine out of ten students drink alcoholic beverages.

Youth in all of the three categories we mentioned earlier are often subject to pressure from their peers and others to use drugs, usually because these individuals will either benefit financially from pushing drugs or because they want to have company in their drug habit. By compiling in one publication information from a wide variety of sources, this book aims to help youths resist arguments for drug use by presenting convincing points against the use of drugs. The book can provide a welcome alternative to merely saying, "I don't use drugs . . ." The intent of this book is not to dissuade an individual from ever experimenting with a drug but rather to prevent drug misuse and abuse. Whether you are a youth, a parent, a teacher, a counselor, or an older adult concerned about youth, it will help you build a case against drugs.

INTRODUCTION

HOW Drugs Can Affect Your Life covers a wide variety of subjects in the drug and alcohol field to give you a good grasp of the influence of drugs on all aspects of an individual's life such as health, safety and well-being. There are a number of key words in the drug and alcohol field including "education," "prevention," "intervention," "treatment," and "rehabilitation." Although all of these areas of dealing with drugs are considered in the book, the special emphasis is upon "prevention," since in the long run, this approach can greatly reduce the need for intervention, treatment, and rehabilitation.

The need for prevention may well be greater today than ever before. Reduction in funding for drug and alcohol treatment and rehabilitation programs is occurring. This means that youths addicted to drugs will not have the same resources for help that previously existed. Prevention of addiction assumes growing importance in such circumstances.

Chapter 2 deals with drugs in general. This chapter lists the principal categories of the drugs of abuse and outlines the main characteristics of each – narcotics, depressants, stimulants, hallucinogens, and a miscellaneous group that includes airplane glue, solvents, and aerosols. In this chapter such terms as drugs, drug abuse, drug misuse, and drug addiction are defined.

Fetal alcohol syndrome is described in Chapter 5. On those pages, the latest information is outlined emanating from research about the syndrome. The dangers of the fetus suffering harmful effects from drinking by the mother are spelled out, and information is included to minimize these dangers so that the possibly devastating effects of the syndrome upon the unborn child can be avoided.

Chapter 6 tells about the effects of drugs, alcohol, and smoking upon sex and stresses that drugs and sex do not mix well, although stories to the contrary often circulate, indicating that some drugs are actually aphrodisiacs and promote sexual satisfaction and enjoyment. Heroin abusers, for example, are so intent upon meeting the demands of their habit that they may completely lose interest in such things as sex.

Still another chapter (Chapter 11) concerns such subjects as emergency treatment for drug overdosing and effects of drug abuse on life-style and physical and emotional health. The final chapter discusses community resources for prevention, intervention, treatment, and rehabilitation in controlling drugs.

The aim of the book is to give details about the effects of alcohol and drugs and to point out ways that drug abuse can be prevented.

ACKNOWLEDGMENTS

DEEP appreciation is expressed to the following individuals who reviewed certain sections of this book and made suggestions about them. These individuals are specialists in such areas as smoking and health; drug and alcohol prevention, treatment and rehabilitation; health information, health promotion, health education and communications; and emergency medical care. We are most grateful to them for their help and much indebted to them for many of the stronger points of the book.

Ruth Nelson Allen, Teacher in Special Education, Bucks County Public Schools, Doylestown, Pa.

Peter S. Amenta, Ph.D., Professor and Chairman, Department of Anatomy, Hahnemann Medical College and Hospital, Philadelphia, Pa.

Harry Epstein, Teacher, School District, Philadelphia, Pa.

Ruth Epstein, Teacher, School District, Philadelphia, Pa.

John Mariano, Coodinator, Emergency Medical Care, Department of Public Health, Philadelphia, Pa.

Thomas Meglin, Director, Office of Legislative Plans and Programs, Pennsylvania Department of Health, Harrisburg, Pa.

Al Meltzer, Sports Commentator, WCAU-TV, Philadelphia, Pa.

Paul Orr, M.D., Instructor, Department of Psychiatry, Medical College of Pennsylvania, Philadelphia, Pa.

Eugene Rosenwasser, Ph.D., Instructor, Department of Chemistry, Jefferson Medical College, Philadelphia, Pa.

Harry Sturm, Director, Alcohol Counseling Services, Warminster General Hospital, Warminster, Pa.

Luther L. Terry, M.D., Former Surgeon General, United States Public Health Service.

Peter A. Theodos, M.D., President, County Medical Society, Philadelphia, Pa.

Carol A. Zappasodi, Musician, Philadelphia, Pa.

Special thanks must be extended to Dr. Luther L. Terry for his review of the section on the history of smoking; to John Mariano for his suggestions in regard to emergency medical care; to Harry and Ruth Epstein for their contributions on prevention; to Dr. Paul Orr for his comments on fetal alcohol syndrome and to Dr. Peter Amenta and Dr. Peter Theodos, who served as consultants on the chapter on effects of drugs.

Sincere thanks are also expressed to Constance Newlin and Laura Beth Allen for their assistance in typing correspondence, drafts and chapters, and the final copy.

W.A.A.
N.L.P.
C.D.A.

CONTENTS

HOW DRUGS
CAN
AFFECT YOUR LIFE

Chapter 1

HOW IT ALL BEGAN – DRUGS, ALCOHOL, SMOKING

> A drug potent against all pain and quarrels and charged with the forgetfulness of all trouble; whoever drank this mingled in the bowl, not one tear would he let fall the whole day long, not if mother and father should die, not if they should slay a brother or a dear son before his face and he would see it with his own eyes.

THESE words from Homer's *Odyssey*, written about 1000 BC, are believed to refer to opium. This is just one of many illustrations that drug use is not something new. Drug use and abuse have a long history. Because of the great variety of drugs that are available today and the concern of society about them, some people believe that the drug abuse problem began in the mid-twentieth century. The truth is that the problem has been around for a long time, probably almost as long as man has inhabited the earth.

As the most popular drug of all, alcohol has been widely used throughout the years, and according to the book *Drug Abuse – Escape to Nowhere*, people who lived during the Stone Age were likely familiar with opium, hashish, and cocaine. As long ago as 5000 BC, marijuana was known to the Chinese, and in 2700 BC, during the reign of the Chinese Emperor Shen Neng, the drug was recommended for gout, constipation, and "absent-mindedness."

Use of marijuana as an intoxicant probably did not occur until sometime between the third and fifth centuries BC. Scythians in what is now Siberia gathered in tents to inhale the smoke of the seeds of the burning hemp plant, from which marijuana is concocted.

It is believed that opium also was used by the Sumerians in 5000 BC, and hallucinogenic drugs such as peyote are still taken by Indian tribes in religious ceremonies. Primitive people used hashish, opium, and cocaine to become intoxicated during religious rites, and hashish was sometimes used as an intoxicant by warriors preparing for battle. The smoking of tobacco has a long history traced to the American Indian.

Opium was known to the Egyptians by 1500 BC. During the Greco-Roman period, it was employed to induce sleep and relieve pain. By the beginning of the Christian era, the use of opium as a treatment for coughs and diarrhea had spread to parts of Europe, where it served as a treatment for a number of illnesses and also to alleviate pain and induce sleep. Because opium was used as an agent to treat hysteria at the time of the Renaissance in Europe, it became one of the first drugs to be employed for treating mental illness.

In early Western European history, there is only occasional reference to opium and other drugs, with the exception of alcohol. It seems that drugs were not as common there and were not used as much as by people living in locations where, because of the favorable climate, plants from which drugs are made could be more easily grown.

In addition to its medical purposes, opium since earliest times has been used for totally different reasons – to lessen anxiety, despair, and gloom and to furnish escape from the realities of life. As a pain killer, opium's potential has long been realized, and by the eighteenth century it had a multitude of medical uses. By the 1700s opium was known to the American colonies, where doctors used it as a medicine and also to combat pain in venereal disease, cancer, gallstones, and dysentery. It was also recommended by physicians for relief of diarrhea, vomiting, muscular spasms and spasms that accompany tetanus, and the pain of menstruation and childbirth. A prominent Philadelphia physician, Dr. Benjamin Rush, who was also a signer of the Declaration of Independence and a medical pioneer who labored to find the cause of the great American epidemics of the 1790s, used opium to treat typhus fever. He urged its use for all those fevers where wine is "safe and proper." In 1790, Dr. Rush gave a lecture at the University of Pennsylvania in which he said that he observed "the happiest effects from it in the fevers at the military hospitals of the U.S. during the late war."

During the latter part of the eighteenth century, opium was also prescribed as a topical agent and was rubbed on the abdomen to relieve spasms of the stomach and on the cheek to allay the pain of toothache and dental abscesses. There were numerous other medical uses in those years, some of which are still good medical practice today.

Figure 1. Among the largest producers of illicit opium in the world are three countries of Southwest Asia – Pakistan, Afghanistan, and Iran.

Even though the drug was being widely used as a medicine, doctors did not understand its addictive properties. Two medical papers written at the University of Pennsylvania in the 1790s revealed that the authors knew about certain characteristics of opium and the dangers of the drug in large amounts but were apparently unaware of the possibilities for addiction it possessed.

In one paper the author compared the actions of opium to those of liquor, and the author of the other paper stressed the hazards of drug use in large quantities. Neither of the authors mentioned the addictiveness of the drug.

A few of the early doctors who prescribed opium knew that their patients and others in the community were using the drug for other than medical purposes. For the most part, physicians were unconcerned about this practice. They felt that such use was nothing more than an "appetite" or "habit" that was no special cause for worry.

Although people have always used drugs, they often did so without knowing the consequences. It was sufficient for them to know that a certain drug brought about a feeling of contentment, that it blocked unpleasantness or took away pain. Personal and social consequences were ignored or simply were undetected. Ignorance about the effects of drug use, which has been a characteristic of such use throughout history, was an important factor in promoting the usage of opium.

The use of another drug, marijuana, in North America is linked with the growing of hemp for cloth. Such cultivation first started in the Americas in Chile where the Spanish had introduced hemp in 1611. The first European settlers of the New World were instructed by King James to grow hemp. The British fleet, which was experiencing a rapid expansion at the time, needed the fiber for rope. Among Colonial farmers who grew hemp for cloth was George Washington, and it is likely that its use as a drug was known at that time. Before the Civil War, hemp was an important cash crop in the South, second only to cotton. Many of the workers in the hemp field probably knew of its use as a drug.

In the mid-1800s Dr. W.B. O'Shaughnessy studied marijuana in the treatment of various diseases. He found tincture of hemp to be an effective analgesic, having anticonvulsant and muscle relaxant effects as well. The Ohio Medical Society in 1860 found hemp to be useful in the treatment of a number of diseases and conditions including tetanus, asthma, and bronchitis. Because marijuana was noninjectable and varied greatly in potency and reaction, its favor in medicine eventually declined.

The potential of opium as a painkiller has been known for

Figure 2. The Pushtuns (Pathans) are among the traditional opium producers in Iran.

many years, and by the start of the nineteenth century it had such a variety of uses that it may well have been regarded as a miracle drug. Problems arising from the use of opium were complicated to an even greater extent in the early nineteenth century by the discovery of two opium derivatives – morphine and codeine. Like the parent drug opium, the properties of these drugs were not fully comprehended by doctors. Even those physicians who realized that opium was addictive failed to understand that the derivatives were also dangerous and in some cases even more dangerous than the parent drug. Because morphine is about 10 times more powerful than opium, it has a higher potential for abuse.

It is ironic that eventually one of the prime uses of morphine and codeine was to help people overcome the opium habit. The drug was given to opium users, who abandoned one habit for another even more serious. Although opium and its derivatives are limited in their value as medicine, they are very effective in combating pain, and even today, there are no drugs that do a better job as analgesics.

European traders were responsible for the spread of drugs to the Far East when they introduced opium to China. Tradesmen used opium in much the same way as American frontiersmen used beads and mirrors in trading with the Indians. In the United States, the hypodermic needle hastened the spread of narcotic addiction. Dr. Gabriel Pravaz of France is credited with inventing the first practical metal syringe with a hollow needle. Prior to Dr. Pravaz's invention in 1853, numerous individuals experimented with various items such as quills to inject themselves and others with various substances. First used in this country in 1856, the hypodermic needle was employed during the Civil War to administer morphine in large quantities to soldiers who suffered bullet or other wounds. It was also given to those who were victims of the dysentery that was rampant during the war.

"Soldier's illness," "army disease," and "morphinomania" were terms for the addiction, which was by no means limited to the military personnel. As morphine use engulfed the civilian population, the hypodermic needle was increasingly employed to administer the drug. It became so common, in fact, that syringes were left with patients to use as they pleased to remedy almost every painful condition. Not only was morphine widely used in medical practice, but it could also be easily obtained from non-medical sources.

As a result of the war, the public learned about the social problem of narcotics and also realized that a medical problem had developed in relation to their use. It is unfortunate that this knowledge failed to prevent the marketing of other opiates such as laudanum. Mixed with alcohol, these compounds were often the main ingredients in patent medicines, hawked from medicine show wagons in a carnival atmosphere, sold at corner drugstores, and advertised in mail order catalogs, newspapers, and magazines. Advertisements in boldface type proclaimed the advantages of toothache drops, painkillers, and home cures. Sold under such names as cordials, soothing syrups, and elixirs, these products, which included opium as a main ingredient, found their heaviest users to be upper and middle class women.

During the latter part of the nineteenth century, narcotic abusers were situated in every level of society, even though the dangers of opium were generally known. The United States of those years has been described as a "dope fiend's paradise." There was no great concern over the use of opium, since it was legally sold and the price was low. Opiates and scores of pharmaceutical preparations containing them could be obtained about as easily as the most common over-the-counter preparations today.

At worst, addiction to opium was compared to alcoholism. At least one physician recommended it as a less dangerous substitute for alcohol. With no legal restriction on opium use, it cut across economic and social lines but occurred most often among members of the middle and upper classes. One exception to this was the smoking of opium, since this use of the drug took place mainly among underworld characters and Chinese laborers working on railroad construction. Consequently there was little contact between the smokers of opium and the so-called "opium eaters" of respectable society, who actually took opium in liquid form.

During the nineteenth century, most of the opium consumed in the United States was legally imported. Not only was morphine manufactured as a legal substance, but also opium poppies were grown legally in the United States. Perhaps the earliest reference to this practice was a letter from Dr. Thomas Bond, a Philadelphia doctor, written to a Pennsylvania farmer in 1781 congratulating the farmer on the good and pure quality of the opium and urging him to take care of the seed.

Even before the use of opium had become quite so widespread, accounts of the dangers of the drug appeared in popular magazines and other publications, but these warnings failed to overcome the public apathy that had developed about opium. In the July 1842 edition of the *Knickerbocker,* a New York magazine, William Blair, a young English immigrant, described his experience with the drug: "I knew that for every hour of comparative ease and comfort its treacherous alliance might confer upon me *now,* I must endure days of bodily suffering, but I did not, could not, conceive the mental hell into whose fierce corroding fires I was about to plunge."

It was not until the early 1900s that addiction to opium and its derivatives brought about social action. There was no doubt by that time that the drug could physically and psychologically enslave its user and that the use of opium was not just a frivolous habit. Physicians had started to consider addiction to opium as a syndrome.

In 1914, the Harrison Act was passed by Congress. Passage of the Act was prompted by increasing public concern over the extent of the narcotics problem and the realization that local and state laws were not adequate. Although the act did not make addiction illegal, it attempted to control the production, manufacture, and distribution of narcotic drugs. The law required registration and payment of an occupational tax by all persons who dealt with narcotic drugs. In addition, it specified that only physicians could dispense narcotics and that pharmacists could sell such drugs only upon written prescription.

Even these restricted legal outlets were soon eliminated for the addict. Due to strong negative feeling about drug users, many court decisions rendered soon after the passage of the act had the effect of strictly limiting the role of physicians in prescribing drugs to addicts. These interpretations allowed doctors to dispense drugs to addicts in diminishing quantities to break drug habits, but not in amounts sufficient to maintain such habits. As a result of this fine legal distinction and the practice of overprescribing by some doctors, there were a number of arrests and convictions of physicians. Many doctors discouraged in their efforts to treat addicts gave up the treatment of addiction.

With both legal sources and clinic sources blocked, addicts turned to an underworld market that previously had been only a minor source. Addicts became increasingly involved in crime to pay the high costs of black market narcotics, and in the public mind, opiate addiction and crime were soon linked. Most horrifying to the public were heroin addicts, possibly because of revulsion by many people to the idea of the drug user employing a hypodermic needle.

Whether because of enforcement efforts or other factors, heroin use fluctuated widely. By the middle 1930s, it was estimated that there were about 60,000 heroin addicts in the United States. After World War II, heroin use increased steadily for about 20 years. When this steady increase then surged into what has been termed an epidemic, the number of heroin addicts climbed dramatically. It is now estimated that there are 500,000 to 600,000 heroin addicts in the nation, and this figure actually represents only a fraction of those who have used the drug once or are occasional users.

Beginning in 1919 and continuing into the early 1920s, outpatient clinics were established by local health departments to treat addicts. The therapy used was to dispense narcotics in gradually decreasing dosages, but this approach was severely criticized by those who felt it was wrong to supply addicts with drugs. Eventually, federal officials stepped in to close the facilities, one of the arguments being that the addicts were receiving more drugs than they actually needed and were selling them in the black market.

High security treatment centers for addicts in the criminal justice system were organized, and these had success in temporarily reducing the number of addicts. In recent years, hundreds of methadone clinics have been set up in various parts of the country. Despite the good results attained by these clinics, they were also the object of criticism. Charges were made that methadone, a synthetic opiate developed in Germany during World War II, was merely being substituted as one narcotic for another in much the same way that morphine had been used to treat opium addiction and heroin to break the addiction to morphine. Among the benefits of the methadone maintenance approach to heroin addiction, however, is that this method usually allows the former addicts to secure and keep regular employment.

In the last generation in the United States, the drug problem has been compounded by the development of quite a number of synthetic drugs, which are brought on the market for medical purposes. Not only did barbiturates and amphetamines constitute contributions to medicine when they were introduced, but they also posed a new potential for abuse. It was not long before this potential became reality. A change in the use of drugs at different levels of the population was prompted by the emergence of these and other drugs. Upper and middle class men and women again joined the drug abuse culture as the result of the new pattern.

It was difficult for the public to alter its point of view to understand the widened use of drugs. Accustomed to thinking of the drug abuser as the heroin addict slinking about in a run-down neighborhood, the public found it hard to picture the youth in the middle-class community or the respected housewife in the suburbs as drug abusers. Also it was confusing to compare the problem of the housewife with a barbiturate dependency to that of the heroin addict in the inner city who mugs the elderly to buy heroin.

During the disturbing decade of the 1960s, with its social conflict, the powerful hallucinogen LSD intruded on the scene, and there was growing use of amphetamines, barbiturates, and certain tranquilizers. The White House Conference of 1962 noted the growing abuse of these drugs by high school and college youth, a trend also reported in scores of newspaper and magazine articles. The period also witnessed renewed popularity of one of the oldest of all drugs – marijuana. The focus of protest movements, the war in Vietnam, appeared to be a spawning ground for drug abuse, and many veterans returned home as addicts, as had Civil War veterans 100 years earlier.

Today, the drug abuse problem exists throughout society, and it is not limited to groups that can easily be identified. Because of the great variety of legal and illegal drugs on the market, patterns of drug abuse have grown more complex. Contributing to the difficulty of solving the drug problem is not only the variety of drugs but also the variance among drug abusers. In dealing with the problem, there is growing recognition of the value of an educational rather than a punitive approach, particularly in regard to the nonnarcotic drugs.

ALCOHOL

Before the beginnings of recorded history, man found that certain substances such as malt grains, fruit juices, and honey could be transformed into fermented potions. The strange effects on mind and body of drinking these beverages very likely filled him with surprise and wonderment. He may well have ascribed magical qualities to these liquids in much the same way that the American

Indian reacted when he first tried drinking the liquors of the white man.

Honey may well have been the oldest product used for fermentation according to evidence from Stone Age cultures, although beer made from barley also has strong claims to being the first alcoholic drink. The drinking habit could have originated in several places at about the same time. Alcoholic drinks first made from barley and later from rice may have stemmed from the grain crops in India. Egypt was apparently the source of African barley beer, and South America's drinking habits may have started in the Maya's farming areas.

The art of brewing barley and water is described in clay tablets found in the Nile Valley dating back to 6000 BC. In ancient Persia in 3000 BC, the fermenting of grape juice to make wine was known, and shortly afterward, the method was introduced into Egypt. Many references to alcoholic beverages can be found in the Bible, particularly in the Old Testament, although the turning of water into wine by Jesus, related in the New Testament, is probably the best known of such incidents.

Mead, made of honey-wine, seems to have been among the first alcoholic beverages distilled by man. Over the years, wide use of mead was indulged in by the Vikings and other cultures. It is clear that alcoholic beverages produced from a surprising number and variety of substances grew into an accepted part of most human societies, a role that these beverages have never entirely relinquished.

In the book *Drinking: Alcohol in American Society, Issues and Current Research,* it is pointed out that the use of alcohol has always eventually led to a perplexing situation as people at different times and in different places have attempted to deal with both the positive and negative aspects of drinking. The use of alcohol serves to make people more relaxed and more at ease. Even today, there is probably nothing that is more widely used as a sedative. Ancient Sumerian and Egyptian writings refer to beer as "the joy bringer," and centuries later, Shakespeare described a quart of ale as a "dish for a king." At the same time, the use of alcohol can lead to excesses of abuse, problem drinking, and alcoholism.

Throughout history, there have been numerous efforts to

establish restrictions of one kind or another on drinking through legal, cultural, and religious means. One of the earliest efforts having both legal and religious aspects was the Code of King Hammurabi of Babylon, which dealt with the regulation of sale, the entering or opening of taverns by temple priestesses, and the use of taverns by criminals and conspirators. Punishment for infringements was severe and in some cases consisted of the death penalty.

In Anglo-Saxon England in the eighth century, there were the early beginnings of a licensing system when Ine, King of Wessex, regulated ale booths and stands. Under Edgar, who ruled as King of England from 959 to 975, regulations were issued that concerned the establishing of ale houses, one only being permitted for each village. Another provision of King Edgar's edicts was that drinking horns were required to have pins affixed at certain intervals to control the amount the drinker consumed. This stipulation did not prove to be very effective, since imbibers learned to rearrange the pins to their advantage.

The formation of social clubs that were often linked with heavy drinking dates from about the eleventh century. Under King Olaf Kyrre (The Tranquil) of Norway, the guilds enjoyed their own club houses, and rules about drinking were enforced. One of the rules was that if one of the members permitted more of his beverage to spill on the table than he could cover with his hand, he was subject to a fine. This rule apparently helped to curb waste of the beverage and also aimed to keep drinkers relatively sober.

In England and Scotland, regulations were passed to keep taverns from staying open after certain hours. In some cases, the penalty for those found in the establishment after the curfew was imprisonment.

Rather early in history, efforts were made to prevent certain groups in the population from drinking at all. In ancient Rome, women were prohibited from drinking wine, and a woman found intoxicated without her husband's knowledge was subject to divorce. In the Aztec culture, young men who drank were clubbed to death. The punishment for young women who imbibed was stoning. Unless a person had reached a certain rather advanced age, he or she was not allowed to drink at all unless permission was obtained from a judge.

During the Middle Ages, beer was often brewed by monks who also engaged in a number of other trades and crafts. Almost every monastery had a brew house. Drinking among the clergy was felt to be especially obnoxious, however. Some religious orders then demanded total abstinence among their membership. Eventually the tasks of brewing were taken over by nonchurchmen. Craft guilds or organizations of brewers were eventually formed as brewing developed into a full-fledged industry.

At the time of the Emperor Charlemagne, noblemen were forbidden to sit in judgement when under the influence of alcohol, and there were strict rules about treatment of soldiers who were alcohol abusers. The problem of drinking in the military forces was well recognized, and in the seventeenth century, Gustavos Adolphus of Sweden stopped the distribution of spirits to his soldiers. Because of the difficulties in enforcing the edict, it remained in force for only a decade.

Concern about the health aspects of drinking lagged behind other considerations. Apparently in the interest of the health of the drinker, the Athenians developed a practice of mixing wine with water. As early as the third century, a Roman jurist suggested that drinking be regarded as a medical problem rather than as a legal one. King James of Aragon, who was in power from 1213 to 1276, passed a number of edicts about drinking. One of them called for hospitalization of persons who were chronically drunk.

In the sixteenth century in Bavaria, there was a stipulation that no one should drink more than two pennyworth, a ruling that seemed to have the health of the drinker in mind.

In 1785, Dr. Benjamin Rush, the famed Philadelphia physician who left his influence on many aspects of medicine during the Revolutionary period, gave an accurate description of alcoholism as a disease. He was one of the first, if not the first doctor to become aware that alcoholism is indeed an illness.

In medieval England, alcohol was often the main drink at festivals, parties, and celebrations. The word was, in fact, sometimes used to mean a festival. Beer at that time was a thick, heavy potion that was about as much food as water with a much higher al-

Figure 3. Dr. Benjamin Rush, the famed Philadelphia physician of the Revolutionary period, gave an accurate description of alcoholism as a disease in 1785.

cohol content than today's beer. Not only was this thick, nourishing beverage important in the daily diet of Europeans, but it was also a safer drink than the badly contaminated water of the era.

As the American Colonies became settled, brewing was established as an industry. One of the first breweries was built by William Penn, the founder of Philadelphia, who constructed the brewery at a home he owned at Pennsbury, just north of the city. By the time of the Revolution, the brewing industry had become an important element in the economy.

In much the same way as other groups before them, the Continental Congress was worried about effects of drinking among troops during the war. Efforts aimed at controlling alcoholic beverages paralleled the movement for American independence. The Congress urged that the states reduce their alcohol quotas to soldiers.

Following the Revolutionary period, drunkenness was a much more frequent occurrence. The book *Drinking: Alcohol in American Society – Issues and Current Research* points out that for the most part, the problem of drunkenness was either ignored, tolerated, or even condoned. Records reveal that alcohol was of growing economic importance at the beginning of the nineteenth century, and people who were under the influence of alcohol became a more common sight both on city streets and in country hamlets.

In 1789, the first temperance organization in American was founded by residents of a New England town, who pledged themselves never to drink. Stands against drinking taken by the Presbyterian and Methodist churches in the early 1800s helped to promote the temperance movement, and in 1826, the American Temperance Society, a national organization, was established.

The Civil War served to foster increased public awareness of the harmful effects of alcohol. As had been the case in the Revolutionary War, drunkenness among soldiers alarmed commanding officers in the field as well as the government. In 1862, a strict antidrinking regulation was put into effect for troops, and the sale of alcohol to soldiers by private citizens was also prohibited.

In the twentieth century, the antisaloon and antialcohol campaign, which had gained a foothold in the previous century, grew in power and gathered support among many groups. Numerous seats in state legislatures and Congress were won and lost on the issue of prohibition. Legislated into law in 1920, prohibition remained in effect until 1933. In the first few years, prohibition enjoyed success, and a sharp decrease took place in alcohol consumption. Some drinkers who may well have been on the way to becoming alcoholics accepted that alcohol was illegal and stopped their consumption. For those who wanted to continue to drink, the void represented by the closing of taverns and bars was soon filled by the appearance of speakeasies and illegal alcohol. Organized bootlegging, the related upsurge in crime, and corruption of law enforcement all played a part in the consumption of alcohol by millions of citizens during the years of prohibition. These factors, coupled with the economic difficulties of the Depression, led to the repeal of the legislation in 1933.

The concept of alcoholism as a disease grew in acceptance in the 1930s as increasing numbers of studies were conducted about alcohol. In 1940, the Center for Alcohol Studies at Yale University was organized to conduct research and report on alcohol and alcoholism. Despite the reports on the dangers of drinking released by the Yale Center and other agencies, a steady increase in alcohol consumption and alcoholism occurred.

In 1935, Alcoholics Anonymous was launched by a New York stockbroker and an Ohio surgeon, both of whom had been alcoholics. They founded AA in an effort to help others who suffered from the disease of alcoholism and also as a means of staying sober themselves. First in the United States, and then throughout the world, AA groups were formed, and today it is estimated that there are more than one million members in 92 countries.

AA is a voluntary worldwide fellowship of men and women from all walks of life who meet together to reach and maintain sobriety. The only requirement for membership is a desire to stop drinking. There are no dues for membership in the organization.

The use of alcohol today is a pervasive part of society and culture. Use of alcohol and the difficulties often accompanying drinking are not likely to disappear at any time soon. Recognizing this situation, public policies to prevent problems related to alcohol such as those with health and social effects face difficult barriers. According to a recent report on alcohol and public policy released by the National Research Council, there is evidence that carefully selected programs can reduce problems associated with the misuse of this drug as long as they are carefully aimed and not so grandiose in design as to attempt to change entire life-styles.

As far as efforts to treat alcoholism are concerned, programs of treatment in the military service, in industry, and in government are successful in 65 to 75 percent of all cases. Programs of therapy can only be successful among those who are willing to recognize that they need help, and accept it.

TOBACCO

The practice of smoking tobacco is believed to have started with the American Indians. News of the custom then spread to other places throughout the world, where it eventually was widely adopted. The word *tobacco* may well have been taken from the *Y*-shaped pipe called a tabaco used by the Indians as a device for snuffing tobacco. A hollow reed or cane tube into which tobacco could be stuffed was used by the Aztec Indians for smoking. Other Indians smoked by crushing tobacco leaves and rolling them into cylinders of corn husks or other vegetable wrappers.

Columbus and other early explorers were amazed to observe Indians who carried these small cylinders of dried leaves, or pipes, and who then "drank" the smoke that billowed from them as soon as they were lighted. The Indians were well aware of the strange power that these burning leaves wielded over them. When English sea captains prevailed upon three Indians to travel with them to London, the Indians, dependent upon the smoking habit, brought their smoking paraphernalia with them. Crews aboard ships of exploration tried the smoking custom and became so enthralled with the habit that they found they craved smoking whenever they were deprived of it.

Long before Indians started the practice of smoking tobacco in the Western Hemisphere, man was smoking concoctions other than tobacco. Done for ceremonial or other reasons, the smoking of these substances, however, did not become a widespread custom. On the other hand, the practice of smoking tobacco developed into a popular habit. Then as today, the nicotine in the tobacco provided an intoxicating effect, making it difficult to quit.

Within a few years after the voyages of Columbus and other explorers and the introduction of tobacco into Europe, the tobacco plant was being cultivated along worldwide trading routes. Magellan's crews smoked tobacco and left seeds in the Philippines and other places where they made port. The Dutch brought tobacco to the Hottentots, and the Portuguese brought it to the Polynesians. The Portuguese, in fact, started the planting of tobacco wherever they had developed trading posts. In many cases, small tobacco farms grew into plantations, often under native control. Before long, almost everywhere sailors traveled – to Asia, Africa, even Australia – they found tobacco was available. The natives learned to smoke as they took care of the tobacco crops.

Among the early uses of tobacco was its fashioning into crude cigars. It is thought that Spanish beggars were the first people to make a type of smoke similar to present day cigarettes. During the early 1500s, beggars on the streets of Seville reportedly picked up cigar butts from the gutters, shredded the butts, and rolled the shreds into scraps of paper. These roughly fashioned smokes were known as "papeletes" or "cigarillos." By the late 1700s, beggars were no longer the only users of cigarillos. They had become respectable and had spread from Spain to Italy, Portugal, Russia, and the Middle East.

During Napoleon's Spanish campaign of 1814, British and French troops learned to smoke cigarillos. Napoleon himself detested the smoking of tobacco, although he became an avid tobacco chewer. Later, a smaller, milder form of the Spanish cigarillo was introduced into France and given the name cigarette. In the Crimean War, British soldiers commenced using Turkish cigarettes with the result that the smoking custom was transported to all of the far-flung places where the troops traveled.

Even as early as the seventeenth century, tobacco was greeted with strong opposition. In 1604, King James II of England declared smoking to be "loathsome to the eye, hateful to the lungs and the black, stinking fumes thereof, nearest resembling the horrible, stigian smoak of the pit that is bottomless."

Louis XIII of France heartily supported this observation, and Czar Michael of Russia threatened early users of tobacco with having their noses slit for the first offense and with death for repeated violations. Pope Urban VIII issued a formal bull against tobacco smoking sealed with the Fisherman's Ring in 1642, and Pope Innocent X followed with a similar edict in 1650. However, many members of the clergy as well as layman continued to smoke.

Smoking was prohibited in Bavaria in 1652, in Saxony in 1653, and in Zurich in 1667. Even the threat of death and the actual putting of the threat into practice failed to stop the smoking habit. Sultan Murad IV decreed the death penalty for offenders in Constantinople in 1633. Wherever he went on military forays, his appearance was accompanied by an astounding increase in executions.

He apparently took a special delight in surprising men in the act of smoking. Punishment consisted of beheading, hanging, or quartering, or in some cases the hands and feet of smokers were crushed and they were left helpless between the lines of battle.

In the United States, tobacco was first used in the form of cigars and for chewing as snuff. John Rolfe, best known for marrying the Indian princess Pocahontas, brought tobacco cultivation to the Virginia Colony about 1612. Local authorities were opposed to the cultivation of the tobacco leaf, however, because farmers chose to grow it for profit rather than using their fields for badly needed food crops. Doctors of those years included tobacco in their bags of medicine, which were meager at best.

It was not until the twentieth century that cigarette smoking became a widespread habit in the United States. The smoking custom was given impetus by both world wars, particularly World War II, when thousands of servicemen who had never smoked before learned the habit in barracks and aboard ship.

Many people who began to smoke during these conflicts had no idea that the habit was harmful to health and looked upon it as something completely innocuous. Even in those years, however, there were some zealots who questioned the safety of smoking and took action against the habit. Among their efforts were presentations in churches and schools, where they made such demonstrations as blowing tobacco through a handkerchief. They pointed out that since tobacco left a dark stain on a piece of cloth, it must be damaging to the tender tissues of the body. It has only been in the last 25 years, however, that scientific evidence has been gathered clearly linking cigarette smoking with poor health and early death.

In 1936, while he was a professor of surgery at Tulane University, Dr. Alton Ochsner called attention to the increasing number of lung cancer cases among Americans and suggested that cigarette smoking might be a major factor. With Dr. Michael DeBakey, he published an article about smoking and its possible relationship to lung cancer, which appeared in the *American Journal of Surgery* in 1939. Dr. Ochsner,who died in October of 1981, continued to oppose smoking as a health hazard throughout his life.

At about the same time, Wynder and Graham at Washington University, St. Louis, expressed concern about the possibly harmful effects of smoking. Later the work of Dr. Daniel Horn and Dr. Cuyler Hammond in the United States and studies in England added more evidence about the health damaging effects of smoking.

In 1956, a joint study was done by the National Cancer Institute, the National Heart Institute, and the American Heart Association concerning the health effects of smoking. The study indicated that smoking was the principal cause of lung cancer and that it was probably involved in cardiovascular and certain lung illnesses. As a result of this study, Surgeon General Leroy Burney in 1957 took an official position for the Public Health Service in regard to smoking and lung cancer. In November of 1959, he published an article in the *Journal of the American Medical Association* clearly stating his position.

On 1 June 1961, a letter was sent to President John F. Kennedy by the presidents of the American Cancer Society, American Heart Association, the American Public Health Association, and the National Tuberculosis Association (now the American Lung Association) pointing out the accumulating evidence on the subject and urging the formation of a presidential commission to study the matter and report to the government and the public.

The president decided that since this was a public health matter it should be the responsibility of the surgeon general. He assigned the responsibility to Surgeon General Luther L. Terry, who then provided for the establishment of an Advisory Committee and supported its activities until the final report was prepared.

On 11 January 1964, Dr. Terry released the report that labeled smoking a health hazard of sufficient importance to warrant remedial action. The report stated that cigarette smoking contributes substantially to the death rate and linked the smoking of cigarettes to cancer, heart disease, ulcers, chronic bronchitis, and emphysema, some of which are among the leading causes of death in the United States.

The release of the report triggered a variety of efforts to make people aware of the dangers of smoking and help them break the smoking habit or at least reduce their smoking. Among these were actions taken to determine the role and responsibility of these agencies in dealing with the problem.

In 1965, the Cigarette Labeling Act was passed. This action not only represented the first official acknowledgement by Congress of the problem but also required the first health warning on cigarette packages and advertising. The ruling of the Federal Communications Commission in 1967 required that the "Fairness Doctrine" previously applied only to political issues should also prevail in the cigarette smoking controversy. This opened the way for the antismoking television messages prepared by the voluntary health associations and the Public Health Service,which proved to be highly effective in alerting the public to the smoking hazards. In 1970, this ruling became moot when Congress revised the smoking act and barred cigarette advertising from the broadcast media.

Over the past few years, there has been increasing concern about the rights of the nonsmoker and the growing realization of the polluting effects of cigarettes especially in offices, passenger cars, and other enclosed spaces. Early in 1982, the Tobacco Institute, a lobbying group for the tobacco industry, launched a series of advertisements questioning studies that have shown smoking to be harmful to health, just as they had argued since the 1964 report.

Today, almost 20 years after the release of the Surgeon General's Report, scores of programs, both legislative and educational, have been developed across the nation to reduce smoking and protect nonsmokers. Despite the staggering evidence compiled by the Surgeon General's Report and thousands of additional studies including the 1982 updating of Dr. Terry's report supporting the original findings and adding more details about the harmful effects, about 52 million Americans are still smoking.

It is known that smoking is harmful not only to the smoker but also to the nonsmoker, that smoking is addictive in the same sense as heroin and alcohol, and that more details are accumulating about the harm that smoking by a pregnant woman can produce in her unborn infant.

More than 30 million people including 100,000 doctors have kicked the smoking habit, and an estimated 90 percent of current smokers want to quit. This is reflected in the annual Smoke-Outs conducted by the American Cancer Society. At the fifth annual Smoke-Out held in November 1981, the Society claimed that 35 percent of the nation's 52 million smokers did not light up, indicating that Americans have a tremendous interest in ridding themselves of the habit. Some smokers who quit for the day manage to stay off cigarettes for good.

A variety of agencies including state and local health departments and voluntary health organizations such as cancer, heart, and lung associations are cooperating in the antismoking endeavor. Optimists in the smoking and health field compare the smoking eradication efforts with the campaign in the early 1900s to outlaw spitting in public places. They predict the day when there will be a smokeless generation, and cigarette lighters and other smoking paraphernalia will join the brass spittoon as relics of the past.

Alan K. Jonas, Chairman of the Board of the American Cancer Society, put it this way, "It may take a generation for it to happen, but the time is coming when the cigarette will go the way of the spittoon, the buggy whip and sasparilla!"

Chapter 2

WHAT DRUGS ARE ALL ABOUT

IF you are ever in a pharmacy when the pharmacist places his order with a drug company, you will probably be amazed at the variety of names he calls off – Demerol®, Pabalate®, Sintrom®, Dilantin®, Orinase®, Aldomet®, Choloromycetin®, Nembutal®, Isordil®, Thorazine®, to name but a few.

What is your reaction when you hear the word *drugs*? Do you think about the many beneficial aspects of drug use, or is your reaction one of concern about the harmful effects when drugs are not used as they should be? As a Public Affairs pamphlet points out, for many people the word *drugs* is emotionally charged and conjures up a frightening image, because for these individuals, the word has become synonymous with drug abuse, drug addiction, and drug problems in general.

Other people think of drugs mainly as being beneficial. Without drugs, numerous individuals, such as recovered heart patients, cancer patients, and those recovered from other diseases, who are now alive and well and going about their daily activities much as they did before they became sick, would be ill, unable to function, or might even have died. Of course, there are still other people who think of drugs as a means of getting away from reality into the world of drug abuse.

The manufacture of drugs is big business in the United States today. Some drugs are produced to be dispensed by pharmacists on prescription from doctors. Others are made to be sold over the counter at corner drugstores, supermarkets, and convenience stores. Millions of people of all ages take drugs for a variety of diseases and conditions. These illnesses include high blood pressure, heart problems, vascular difficulties, kidney disorders, diabetes, epilepsy, chronic bronchitis, back pain, and even such minor complaints as the common cold.

In recent years, hundreds of new drugs have been introduced for inducing sleep and for tranquilization, sedation, and relief of pain, motion sickness, and allergy symptoms. Too numerous to list, they include narcotics, barbiturates, other hypnotic-sedative drugs, the benzodiazepines, and antihistamines. In many cases, the drugs are used as they should be, and they contribute immeasurably to improve the health, welfare, and safety of uncounted numbers of people.

In other instances, however, the drugs are not used as intended, with damaging effects to the individual and society. It is evident today that drug misuse and abuse is a widespread problem in our society. Some people have the idea that at least part of the reason for drug misuse lies in the pressures of society such as the goals we set for ourselves and pursue. Others are of the opinion that it lies principally with the individual and that he or she is somehow at fault. Still others are convinced that some combination of these reasons is responsible for the permeation of every level of society with drug abuse and misuse. Before the problems with drug and alcohol misuse can be surmounted, there must be widespread understanding among the general public about the nature and extent of the drug problem.

You as an individual can learn as much as possible about drugs, face up to the drug issue, and come to grips with it. You can make an informed choice, not an ignorant one. If you decide that drugs are not for you, you can help create an environment that will make it easier for you and others to avoid becoming abusers or misusers of drugs.

Before we go any further, the question should be answered, Just what is a drug? For the purposes of this book, a drug is any substance that by its chemical nature alters the structure or function of the individual taking the drug. A drug, in fact, is any chemical substance that changes mood, perception, or consciousness of the individual or has a harmful effect on society, or both.

Drugs consist of natural as well as synthetic chemical substances. The use of drugs can affect your body and its processes, your mind and nervous system, and your behavior and feelings. When properly used to treat a medical problem, drugs can accomplish a number of beneficial results. These include correcting imbalances in body chemistry, furnishing protection against illness, combating organisms that have invaded the body, and lessening tension, fatigue, and pain.

On the other hand, the abuse of drugs can lead to many serious problems. Each year, almost a quarter of a million people are treated in hospitals for drug-related accidents and mental and physical illness. In addition thousands of people die annually as the result of drug abuse. Costs of drug abuse are high not only to the individual but also to society. For the individual, costs range from a dollar or two a day for cigarettes to well over $100 a day for heroin and even higher amounts for cocaine. Costs to society in terms of lost productivity and medical and other expenses are estimated to be more than $100 billion yearly.

Still another aspect of drug abuse is that at least a half million people are arrested each year for drug-related offenses. Unfortunately, drugs users who become addicted often resort to increasing use of drugs. They choose this dangerous route rather than obtaining help through drug treatment agencies and other organizations to solve their problems.

It is almost impossible for an individual to do something to himself that only affects him. Eventually, it seems, any action will have influence upon these who are close to him, such as parents, brothers and sisters and others who depend upon him. There are also effects upon society. Victims of drug abuse who become physically or emotionally disabled are usually completely dependent upon society for subsisting. This means that society picks up the tab for the individual's living expenses as well as for treatment and rehabilitation. Beyond that, a drug dependent person is a human loss to himself, his family, and his community.

There are four general categories of drugs of abuse, each having certain characteristics. There is also a category comprising a miscellaneous grouping.

Narcotics are opium derivatives, which are also referred to as "opiates." The narcotics are addicting. They are used to relieve pain. Included in the category are opium, heroin, morphine, codeine, and synthetics like methadone and Demerol.

Depressants are also referred to as sedatives. They depress the central nervous system and can lead to addiction. This category includes alcohol, barbiturates (sleeping pills), and some tranquilizers including the benzodiazepines such as Valium® and Librium®.

Stimulants stimulate the central nervous system and accelerate body processes, often to a dangerous degree. The stimulants also produce a false sense of well-being, which may be followed by severe depression. Included in this category are pep pills, some weight reduction pills, methamphetamines (speed), and cocaine.

Hallucinogens are mind-altering drugs that can produce hallucinations. The category of halluginogens includes LSD, PCP, peyote and STP. We include marijuana here also.

Inhalants, also known as deliriants make up a miscellaneous grouping of chemicals including airplane glue, solvents, aerosols, and other substances. Some of these chemicals can cause irreversible damage to the brain and other organs when ingested or inhaled.

As we will stress a number of times in this book, alcohol is a drug – one that is used often by a great many people. Ethyl alcohol is produced by the action of yeast cells upon carbohydrates in grains and fruit. There are three types of alcoholic beverages that are commonly made – beers, wines, and distilled liquors, which are sometimes called spirits. Beers are fermented from grains and contain 3 to 6 percent alcohol. Beers of varying flavors include ale, porter, and stout.

Wines are fermented from fruits. Ordinarily they contain 12 to 14 percent alcohol, although fortified wines have additional alcohol added, which raises the alcohol content to 18 to 20 percent. Liquors are made from distilled or boiled off alcohol and contain 40 to 50 percent alcohol, expressed in degrees of proof. One proof equals ½ percent of alcohol. For example, whiskey, gin, rum, brandy, and vodka are types of liquors. Cocktails and highballs are liquors distilled with fruit juice and soda water.

In thinking about the action of drugs, facts that should be considered are the action of the drug on the body and the action of the body on the drug. Dr. Wolfgang Vogel of Jefferson Hospital in Philadelphia says that we usually consider a drug as only having an effect upon the body. It should be kept in mind that the body also affects the drug and greatly alters its characteristics and determines outcomes and how long the drug action lasts. Comments made by Dr. Vogel at a lecture series on drugs held in Philadelphia have been incorporated into this chapter.

Depending upon our emotional state, we can perceive the effect of a particular drug differently. For instance, if we are tired, a bottle of beer might make us sleepy. In a social setting such as at a party, the same bottle of beer might serve to stimulate us. Environmental influences play a part in the determination of emotional state and influence drug action.

When a drug is used, a real effect is generally experienced by everyone. An imagined effect can vary from one person to another depending upon his or her psychological make-up.

The Food and Drug Administration defines drug use as the "taking of a drug for its intended purpose in the appropriate amount, frequency, strength and manner." Drug misuse is "taking a substance for its intended purpose, but not in the appropriate amount, frequency, strength or manner." Drug abuse is "deliberately taking a substance for other than its intended purpose and in a manner that can result in damage to the person's health or his ability to function." As mentioned earlier, drug abuse can have harmful effects upon the community, thus encompassing far more than harm solely to the individual or even to his close friends and family.

Drug action is determined by several factors, including the chemical structure of the drug. Barbiturates and amphetamines produce different effects because they have different chemical structures. Changing a drug's chemical structure can greatly alter its effects. Another factor influencing drug action is the dosage. A certain amount of a drug must be taken for a particular effect to take place. For example, taking one-fourth of an aspirin pill to alleviate a headache brings no results. Taking two pills, however, will probably cause the headache to disappear. Three dozen pills will lead to an overdose reaction.

The drug must also be available in a form the body can use. A few years ago, a drug was marketed contained in plastic capsules. Because these capsules would not dissolve in the stomach, the patient would simply excrete the undissolved pills. As a result, not any of the active drug would ever reach the patient's bloodstream. Drugs must be manufactured in such a way that they are available to the body.

Certain drugs must be administered in a specific way for a given effect to result. To illustrate, some drugs must be injected to produce beneficial effects. If they are given orally, the drugs are broken down in the stomach before desired effects are produced. The method by which the drugs are introduced into the body influences the onset of action. Intravenous administration usually furnishes the quickest action.

Sometimes dosage such as a time capsule is used to prolong drug action beyond the time of a single dose. The place of application may be far removed from where it acts. For example, a medication taken by mouth may be used to heal an infection of the toenail. Dr. Steven Teti, a pharmacist, points out that drugs include active and inactive ingredients. The active ingredients in a large pill may be so small it can be placed on the point of a pencil. The active ingredient may be distributed throughout the pill or it may be lodged in a central core. Inactive ingredients include such things as the coating of the tablet.

Absorption and distribution are important factors in determining the onset and duration of drug action. One example is a drug taken orally. After the drug is swallowed, it goes into the stomach and has to dissolve in the stomach. Next, the drug is absorbed through the stomach and intestine into the bloodstream. The blood then carries the drug to all the tissues throughout the body.

All drugs can be harmful, particularly if they are abused or misused. Even over-the-counter drugs can be used habitually or in a reckless way. The effect of any drug depends upon a number of factors, some of which have already been mentioned. Among the factors are how often the drug is taken and the route of use which in the case of a drug of abuse might be smoking, sniffing, or skin popping, and the use in connection with other drugs. Among other factors are a person's experience with the drug, his personality, what he expects to derive from taking the drug, and the surroundings in which it is used. A drug taken in a hospital might have one effect, while the same drug taken illicitly at a teenage party could have an entirely different effect.

Through continued use of certain drugs, people may become addicted to them. Drug addiction, often termed drug dependence, results from continuous or periodic use of a drug. When the effects produced by a drug have become necessary for an individual's well-being, he has become psychologically dependent upon the drug. This dependence can be characterized by behavior withdrawal, that is, by drug-seeking behavior caused by a compulsion to use the drug.

Physical dependence occurs only if withdrawal symptoms show up when a person stops using the drug. Withdrawal symptoms occur as a physical reaction, such as vomiting, muscle tremors, and aches and pains, and are not psychological, but the two are sometimes very hard to separate. An addicted and drug-dependent person using certain drugs usually builds up a tolerance to the drug. This means that he or she must have increasingly larger amounts of the drug to obtain the same effect.

Addiction to drugs may occur in the case of a person who begins experimenting with drugs and then becomes dependent upon them. It may also take place when a person who is taking a prescribed drug becomes addicted to it. An example of the latter would be a youth who is given a pain-killing drug to deaden the pain from a leg broken in a skiing accident and who then becomes addicted to the drug.

The question is repeatedly raised, however, Why do people, particularly youth with all of life ahead of them, persist in drug abuse, when it can lead to so many serious problems?

It seems that there are a variety of reasons for drug abuse today. They range from the belief that all problems, whether physical or mental, can be solved by medication, to widespread access to various drugs, "peer pressure," and the enjoyment of the effects of drugs. The family medicine chest may be the first place to which children turn as a source of drugs that can be misused. In many homes the medicine chest is actually a stockpile of drugs. To reduce the danger of the medicine chest being used as a drug source for abuse and misuse, all family members should resort to drugs only as prescribed. In addition, drugs should be disposed of when no longer needed. Doctors and pharmacists can assist by carefully checking renewal of prescription drugs that can cause dependence.

Reasons for experimenting with drugs such as curiosity or peer pressure may be a lot different from the reasons people decide to use drugs regularly. Among reasons for the latter decision are social acceptance and the enjoyment supposedly produced by drugs. Emotional dependence or fear of the effects of withdrawal are among the reasons people continue to use drugs on a regular basis.

The booklet *Drug Abuse in a Chemical Dependent Society* quotes a government survey among college drug users who gave the following reasons for their use of drugs:

To feel less afraid or more courageous
To find out more about oneself
To have a religious experience or come closer to God
To satisfy a strong craving or compulsion
To relieve boredom
To increase or reduce appetite
To feel less dull or sluggish
To improve sex
To reduce sexual desire
To keep from being panicked or going crazy
To feel less depressed or sad
To relieve tension or nervousness
To make a good mood last longer
To relieve anger or irritability
To make one more friendly or loving toward others
To commit suicide
To improve intelligence or learning
To improve physical performance

Another study of youthful addicts in New York City aimed at learning about the characteristics of the families of which they were members. Five points were compiled:

Absent or weak father
Overprotective, overindulgent, and domineering mother
Inconsistent standards of behavior set by parents
Hostility or conflict between parents
Unrealistic aspiration for children

An increasing trend is the phenomenon of multiple drug use now being noted. Termed the polydrug syndrome, this practice develops when the user's preferred drug is not available or in short supply. According to authorities, 75 percent of patients in drug treatment programs routinely use two or more drugs either simultaneously or in sequence. It is not unusual for a heroin addict to be an alcoholic, and the heavy amphetamine user may skip to heroin, cocaine, hallucinogens, and alcohol as well.

This is not to say that the use of one drug automatically leads to a more powerful or more dangerous drug. It nevertheless raises the question whether youths who start with such a common drug as alcohol usually go on to other drugs, including the narcotics. A St. Louis study showed that two-thirds of the men who ever used drugs first used them in their teens or earlier. Adolescent users more often went on to heroin use and addiction than did those who began drug use in their 20s. Although heroin was almost always preceded by marijuana use, only a minority of marijuana users went on to try heroin. In fact, almost half of the drug users reported using only marijuana.

Of course, there are even greater dangers to the drug abuser when a combination of drugs is taken. This is particularly true of alcohol and barbiturates (sleeping pills), which represent the combining of two sedative drugs. There are also special hazards when a stimulant is combined with a sedative by the abuser in an effort to obtain a roller coaster effect. Such apparently was the case in the death of comedian John Belushi. According to a medical examiner's report, the comedian died of a heroin-cocaine overdose.

Many treatment programs are available for the drug abuser today, and these programs can be found in large and small communities across the entire nation. The number and variety of these programs have been steadily increasing in recent years as the drug problem has burgeoned. Funding cutbacks that began to show up late in 1981 may deter this growth, but up until that time, just about anybody who sought treatment could find it, particularly in large cities.

Because no single approach seems to be successful for all drug abusers, several types of treatment are furnished. For drugs other than alcohol, these programs basically include methadone maintenance and therapeutic programs. In methadone maintenance, which is available only to the heroin abuser, the patient receives prescribed doses of methadone, a synthetic narcotic, together with a wide range of social support services to aid in rehabilitation. Drug-free programs accessible to both heroin and other drug abusers may have outpatient programs giving a wide variety of services or live-in locations where patients are residents. About one out of three patients in federally funded programs is in a methadone program, while the rest are in drug-free programs. Alcohol treatment services include supportive treatment through groups such as Alcoholics Anonymous, Al-Ateen and Al-Anon for family members or friends of the alcoholic. A success rate of 65 to 75 percent is achieved in treatment programs for alcoholics. Success rates for other drug abusers are not as high, being in the range of an estimated 15 to 30 percent.

Addiction is commonly associated with the use of heroin, a drug that is feared by the general public more than any other. In the United States, however, a greater number of people are addicted to benzodiazepines than to opiates, and withdrawal from depressants is more severe and dangerous than withdrawal from heroin. All drugs can be psychologically addicting; opiates, barbiturates, and other depressants can also produce physical dependence.

The National Clearinghouse for Alcohol Information warns that because alcohol works on the same brain areas as certain drugs, it can add to the usual responses ordinarily expected from either the drug or the alcohol alone. For example, alcohol and barbiturates in combination increase each other's effects on the central nervous system and can be especially dangerous, since they both have a sedating effect, a result known as synergism.

In fact, alcohol in combination with any drug that has a depressant effect on the central nervous system also represents a special hazard to health and safety and can even be a threat to life itself. To explain this reaction, it is necessary to have an understanding of metabolism – the way our bodies chemically process those things we eat, drink, or take as a medication or for some other purpose.

If drugs were not metabolized within the body, their effects would continue for the remainder of a person's life. Through the metabolic process, drugs are transformed to other substances and eventually eliminated through normal body processes. Generally, a quickly metabolized drug has less dangerous impact. When certain drugs are forced to compete with alcohol to be processed by the body, alcohol is metabolized first, while the other drug remains active in the body for a long time. As a result, the drug's effect on the body is exaggerated, since its metabolism is slowed down due to the body's tendency to take care of the alcohol first. When added to the normal depressant consequences of alcohol, there occurs further depression of the nervous system, which regulates body functions – a serious condition that can lead to death. There is yet another danger, which can result in serious problems in persons who habitually drink large amounts of alcohol. As a result of excessive drinking, barbiturates and other depressants will have less effect. Consequently, it is not uncommon for heavy drinkers to take even larger doses of certain drugs (depressants) because tolerance to them is accelerated by chronic alcohol use. The results of taking the larger doses and then drinking can place these persons in even greater jeopardy and can be fatal. The results of taking the larger doses and then drinking can place these persons in even greater jeopardy and can be fatal.

The National Clearinghouse for Alcohol Information urges you to think before you drink. If you want to take a drink when you are also taking medication, the Clearinghouse advises three actions on your part may save you from a serious illness or may even save your life. (1) Read the warnings on nonprescription drug labels and those on your prescription on container. (2) Ask your doctor about possible alcohol/drug interactions. (3) Check with your pharmacist if you have any questions about your medication, especially those you can buy without a doctor's prescription.

WHAT COULD HAPPEN IF YOU DRINK WHILE TAKING ANY OF THESE DRUGS

The following list which has been prepared by the Clearinghouse lists classes of drugs that have been reported to interact with alcohol. Some of the dangers that may result from combining alcohol with the other listed drugs are described. The Clearinghouse emphasizes that this list, or any like it, only represents the smallest part of the whole alcohol/drug interaction picture. It is not meant to replace the advice of your family doctor or your pharmacist. Further information about any of the items included in the list may by obtained from the National Clearinghouse for Alcohol Information (see Chapter 12).

Analgesics, narcotic
(Demerol®, Darvon®, Dilaudid®, etc.)
When used alone, both alcohol and narcotic drugs cause a reduction in the function of the central nervous system. When used together, this effect is even greater and may lead to loss of effective breathing function (respiratory arrest). Death may occur.

Analgesics, nonnarcotic
(Aspirin, APC®, Pabalate®, etc.)
Even when used alone, some nonprescription pain relievers can cause bleeding in the stomach and intestines. Alcohol also irritates the stomach and can aggravate the bleeding especially in ulcer patients.

Antialcohol preparations
(Antabuse®, calcium carbamide)
Use of alcohol with medications prescribed to help alcoholic patients keep from drinking results in nausea, vomiting, headache, high blood pressure, and possible erratic heart beat, and can result in death.

Anticoagulants
(Panwarfin®, Dicumarol®, Sintrom®, etc.)
Alcohol can increase the ability of these drugs to stop blood clotting, which in turn can lead to life-threatening or fatal hemorrhages.

Anticonvulsants
(Dilantin®, Diphenyl®, EKKO®, etc.)
Drinking may lessen the ability of this drug to stop convulsions in a person.

Antidepressants
(Trofanil®, Pertofrane®, Triavil®, etc.)
Alcohol may cause an additional reduction in central nervous system functioning and lessen a person's ability to operate normally. Certain antidepressants in combination with red wines like Chianti may cause a high blood pressure crisis.

Antidiabetic agents/hypoglycemics
(Insulin®, Diabenese®, Orinase®, etc.)
Because of the possible severe reactions to combining alcohol and insulin or the oral antidiabetic agents, and because alcohol interacts unpredictably with them, patients taking any of these medications should avoid alcohol.

Antihistamines
(most cold remedies, Actifed®, Coricidin®, etc.)
Taking alcohol with this class of drugs increases their calming effects and a person can feel quite drowsy, making driving and other activities that require alertness more hazardous.

Antihypertensive agents
(Serpasil®, Aldomet®, Esidrix®, etc.)

Alcohol may increase the blood pressure lowering capability of some of these drugs, causing dizziness when a person gets up. Some agents will also cause a reduction in the function of the central nervous system.

Antinfective agents/antibiotics
(Flagyl®, Chloromycetin®, Seromycin®, etc.)
In combination with alcohol, some may cause nausea, vomiting, and headache, and possibly convulsions, especially those taken for urinary tract infections.

Central nervous system stimulants
(most diet pills, Dexedrine®, caffeine, Ritalin®, etc.)
Because the stimulant effect of this class of drugs may reverse the depressant effect of the alcohol on the central nervous system, these drugs can give a false sense of security. They do *not* help intoxicated persons gain control of their movements.

Diuretics
(Diuril®, Lasix®, Hydromox®, etc.)
Combining alcohol with diuretics may cause reduction in blood pressure, possibly resulting in dizziness when a person stands up.

Psychotropics
(Tindal®, Mellaril®, Thorazine®, etc.)
Alcohol and the "major tranquilizers" cause additional depression to central nervous system function, which can result in severe impairment of voluntary movements such as walking or using the hands. The combination can also cause a loss of effective breathing function and can be fatal.

Sedative hypnotics
(Doriden®, Quaalude®, Nembutal®, etc.)
Alcohol in combination further reduces the function of the central nervous system, sometimes to the point of coma or the loss of effective breathing (respiratory arrest). This combination can be fatal.

Sleep medicines
It is likely that nonprescription sleeping medicines, to the degree that they are effective, will lead to the same kind of central nervous system depression when combined with alcohol as the minor tranquilizers (see below).

Tranquilizers – minor
(Miltown®, Valium®, Librium®, etc.)
Tranquilizers in combination with alcohol will cause reduced functions of the central nervous system, especially during the first few weeks of drug use. This results in decreased alertness and judgment and can lead to household and automotive accidents.

Vitamins
Continuous drinking can keep vitamins from entering the bloodstream. However, this situation changes when a person stops drinking.

Other
If you have come across other drugs that appear to interact with alcohol check with your doctor or pharmicist to be sure.

Chapter 3

HOW DRUGS AFFECT MIND AND BODY

PAUL is an 18-year-old high school student living in Northeast Philadelphia. Popular with boys and girls, he plays baseball and basketball and likes to swim. When he graduates from high school, he plans to study civil engineering. When asked the question what he would like to learn about drugs, he was quick to answer, "What drugs do to you."

His 17-year-old girlfriend Laura is a slender blond with blue eyes. She gets good grades in math and is a member of her high school track team. She hopes to study medical science in college. Her answer to the same question was similar – "I'd like to know the effects of drugs on mind and body."

Millie is an office worker in center-city Philadelphia. She is known for her neatness and the organization of her work. She likes to travel and has been to several countries, including Canada and Portugal. When asked what she would like to know about drugs, her reply was this – "Just what effects do drugs have upon a person's mental abilities?"

George is a youth counselor in the north central part of the city. He likes to jog and play tennis. "I'd like to know the effects of drugs upon kids in their formative years," he responded to the question.

The purpose of this chapter is to answer your questions about drugs, alcohol, and smoking and to give some details about the effects they have upon you, both immediate and long-range.

Many people know that heroin and morphine are drugs, but many do not realize that tobacco is also a drug. Scientific evidence has been accumulating for years showing that tobacco is psychologically addictive and can lead to physical dependence in the same sense as heroin. In mid-1981, the National Institute on Drug Abuse (NIDA) stated that cigarette smoking is addictive in the same sense as heroin and morphine and urged that a blunt warning to that effect be added to the labels of cigarette packages. One of the aims of NIDA is to let young people who are just starting to smoke know that they just can't stop whenever they want to. NIDA states that youths should be aware that tobacco is a drug they just can't fool around with.

Effects of Smoking

Since tobacco has been classified as a drug, let's start by discussing the harmful effects of smoking. By this time, you would think that people have a pretty good idea about the damage that cigarette smoking can cause, but it shouldn't be assumed that everyone knows all the facts. A well-known television commentator who died of lung cancer a few years ago reportedly said when he was told he had lung cancer and that it was probably linked to his heavy smoking, "No one ever told me to stop smoking. I didn't know that it was dangerous."

If this commentator did not have knowledge about the hazards of smoking, it's a good bet that there are many youths and others who don't have all the facts about it. During a health lecture at a university, the lecturer commented that one of the dangers of cigarette smoking is the possibility of the smoker developing cancer of the urinary bladder. One of the students in the class approached the lecturer after the session and asked if he had heard correctly that smoking is a cause of bladder cancer. When he was assured that this is true, he walked away looking worried. He probably knew a lot about the dangers of smoking but had never heard about smoking being linked with bladder cancer, and this fact clearly had special meaning for him.

Speaking at a conference in Philadelphia, Dr. Peter A. Theodos, a member of the Board of Directors of the American Lung Association of Philadelphia and Montgomery County, said that a great number of studies have determined the harmful effects of smoking. These included experiments, clinical and autopsy studies, and population surveys. He pointed out that damage caused by smoking includes the effects of chemicals such as nicotine, carbon monoxide, and cancer-producing agents. Nicotine is a toxic substance that speeds up the cardiovascular system and places an added burden on the heart. Carbon monoxide combines with hemoglobin to make it more difficult for the body to exchange oxygen. Furthermore, the heat of a cigarette, which reaches 1000 degrees Fahrenheit, has a harmful effect upon tissue of the mouth and lips.

What happens when you smoke? The fact is that cigarette smoking can eventually have effects from the top of your head to your big toe, as Figure 4 illustrates. This process can begin in less time than it takes you to read the next line of type. Practically the instant that you inhale tobacco smoke, the poisonous vapor launches its harmful effects upon your heart, your lungs, your entire body. It starts your heart pounding an extra 15 to 25 beats per minute, raises your blood pressure by 10 to 20 points, and, as just pointed out, damages the delicate membranes of your lips and mouth. In your lungs, it chokes the airways and commences an attack upon the tiny air sacs and tubes leaving a residue of cancer-causing chemicals. These and other harmful poisons are deposited in your stomach, your kidneys, and your urinary bladder.

A special kind of x-ray shows that smoking even one cigarette can diminish the flow of blood to the fingers. It's no wonder that the smoking of cigarette after cigarette over several years can lead to serious damage to the tissue of the cardiovascular system and may eventually result in a heart attack or stroke. All of this happens with every single cigarette you smoke. No smoker is immune to the harmful results, although some smokers try to kid themselves into thinking that they are.

A newspaper reporter was assigned to interview a renowned physician who was well known for her opposition to cigarette smoking. While waiting to begin the interview, the reporter lit a cigarette and began to puff happily on it. The doctor, who had known the reporter for many years, commented that he was still smoking cigarettes.

"Yes, and it doesn't bother me a bit," he smiled. The doctor looked him right in the eye and said, "That's what you may think.

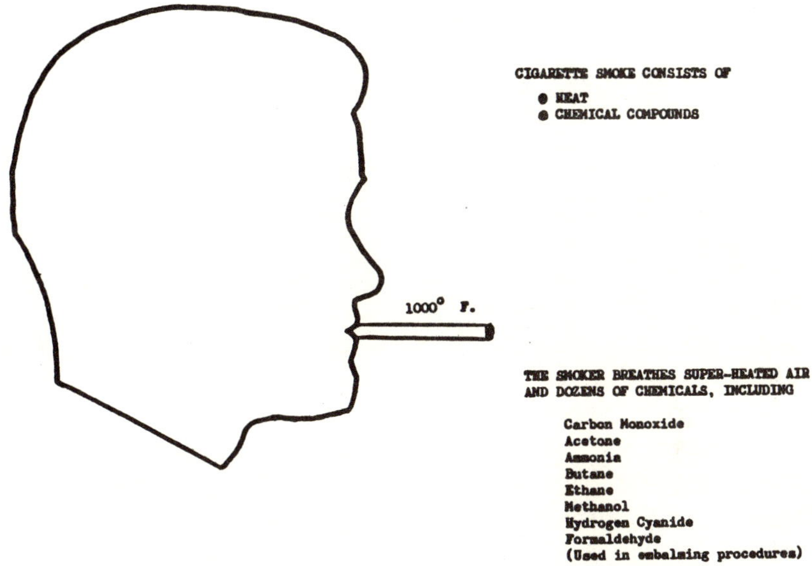

Figure 4. Cigarette smoke consists of heat and chemicals.

Every time you breathe, I hear the wheezing of your chronic bronchitis."

The cheery smile faded from the reporter's face and he crushed out the smoke, which somehow didn't taste as good as it had. The doctor's remarks had struck home. Who could know better than the reporter about the hacking coughing spells he had almost every morning?

If you are a smoker, each time you inhale, you suck into your body smoke containing acids, glycerol, glycol, alcohols, aldehydes, ketones, and phenols, among other chemicals. Among the aldehydes is formaldehyde, used in embalming procedures. These poisons are breathed deeply into your bronchial tree. When you exhale, only about 10 percent of these chemicals are expelled from your body. The remaining 90 percent stay inside your body, where the deposits from the poisonous vapors can eventually cause all kinds of trouble. As we mentioned, the deadly carbon monoxide not only robs your blood of oxygen but also keeps the red cells from giving up oxygen as fast as the tissues demand. What is the result of this deprivation? Because of their smoking, smokers are getting as little oxygen as if they lived at an altitude of about 8,000 feet above sea level. If you are a smoker, your body is getting as little oxygen as if you lived on top of a mountain almost two miles high!

How does lung cancer develop in the smoker? Any smoker who has been puffing away at cigarettes for several years has typical as well as atypical cells in his respiratory tract. Atypical cells are those which are in the process of change. Dr. Peter Amenta of Hahnemann Medical College, who frequently lectures on smoking, illustrates the point as he talks. He starts to tap lightly on the shoulder of one of his listeners, who looks more and more startled as the tapping continues.

"If I don't stop hitting this fellow on the shoulder, he's likely to stand up and punch me on the chin," Dr. Amenta says. "But I'm illustrating the point of what happens when a cell in the respiratory tract is repeatedly subjected to the abuse of cigarette smoke. It will take the abuse just so long and it will then react by turning into a cancer cell."

No one can predict when the change into a cancer cell will occur, but once it does, a localized cancer can develop and over a period of time spread to other parts of the body if not detected and treated. For the heavy smoker who persists in the habit over a period of years, the chances of developing cancer of the lung are about one in ten. Once a person is afflicted with lung cancer, the chances of living for even five years are only about one in twelve. Of course, even if the smoker escapes cancer of the lung, there are a number of other cancers he may fall prey to as well as such other illnesses as heart disease, chronic bronchitis, and emphysema.

Don't think that just because you are young, you can escape the harmful effects of cigarette smoking. Teenage smokers frequently get winded during mild exercise even though they smoke only a half dozen cigarettes or so a day. Every smoker who plays a sport such as football will likely find that he will be out of breath more quickly than his nonsmoking teammates. Other consequences, although not nearly as serious, are stained fingers, unpleasant tobacco breath, and yellowed teeth.

As Dr. Theodos points out, tobacco contains nicotine, which

acts on the heart, the blood vessels, digestive tract, kidneys, and nervous system. It's the nicotine that gives you a "lift," but at the expense of placing extra demands upon your body, particularly upon your heart. People in good health can usually increase their coronary blood flow enough to meet this demand, but those with coronary heart disease cannot. For this reason, people who have diagnosed heart disease and those with undetected heart disease may be especially susceptible to the harmful effects of smoking. It now seems that smoking can also speed up the formation of blood clots, which suggests another way in which smoking increases deaths from illnesses involving clotting of the blood, such as coronary thrombosis.

Smokers are actually an "at risk" group in the popular sport of scuba diving, the *American Journal of Nursing* reports. Smokers inhale air with a lower oxygen content and a higher proportion of carbon dioxide and assorted irritants than do nonsmokers, the article states. The irritants can inflame and swell the mucous membranes interfering with the air passages during a dive and impeding the interchange of gas. Smokers who dive are also more likely to suffer from a stupor or even from unconsciousness than are nonsmokers. The article adds that smokers with decreased pulmonary function should be encouraged to give up smoking and begin an exercise program to improve heart and lung functioning.

The taste and flavor of your cigarette are produced by the chemicals mentioned earlier. Condensed from smoke, particles from these chemicals form a considerable amount of sticky, smelly tar. If you are a pack-a-day smoker, this means that each year you are inhaling almost a full cup of tar in the smoke from your cigarettes. People who lecture on the dangers of smoking sometimes display jars filled with this kind of tar, and it is indeed a black, gooey substance damaging to the tissue of the respiratory tract, which is one of the most tender and delicate parts of the human body.

If you are a female who is pregnant and you are a smoker, you are smoking for yourself and your unborn baby, which your infant will certainly not appreciate. Nicotine constricts the blood vessels in your unborn child, cutting down on the flow to the fe-

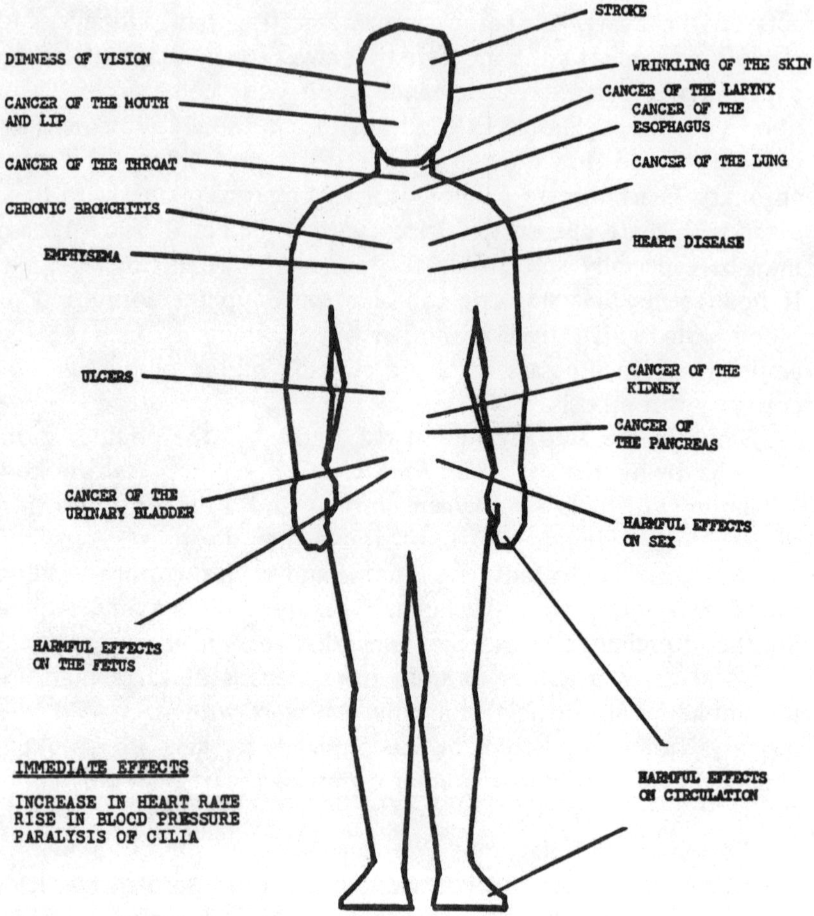

Figure 5. Effects of smoking – from head to toe.

tus, which just can't get enough blood or oxygen to grow as fast as it normally would.

Babies of mothers who smoke during pregnancy weigh an average of six ounces less at birth than those of nonsmoking mothers. This may not sound like much of a weight reduction, but to a baby weighing only five or six pounds, it represents a significant percentage of the total weight. Several studies have revealed that the mother who smokes during pregnancy greatly increases the chances of bearing a premature infant. Since prematurity is a leading cause of infant death, such babies may fail to live until their first birthday. According to a study done in England, many babies are born dead because the mother smoked. The smoking habit, the survey asserts, has a bad effect upon a woman's blood pressure during pregnancy. Smoking mothers also have more miscarriages.

Air pollution is bad news for all of us, but it appears that it is especially bad news for the smoker. Gerhard Angermann, writing in *Air Pollution Control Progress,* a publication of the Philadelphia Department of Public Health, points out that if a nonsmoker gets any foreign matter from polluted air in his lungs, it is pushed back up the bronchial tree by the banks of tiny hair-like structures called cilia on the inner cell lining of the respiratory tract. The mechanism works something like an escalator. When the debris reaches the throat, it is harmlessly swallowed or expectorated.

In the case of the smoker, however the hot gases from cigarettes throw the cleansing mechanism out of kilter. The great heat of at least 1000 degrees Fahrenheit along with the chemicals in the smoke has a paralyzing effect upon the cilia and stops their sweeping action. Some medical researchers say that the nicotine is also guilty in the breakdown of the cleansing process. At any rate, the escalator stops, and all the debris that would have been escalated out of the lungs now piles up on the inner surfaces, which are made up of thousands of tiny air sacs called alveoli. For the smoker, this is a double dose of pollution: debris from his own cigarette smoke and debris from the dirty air he breathes between puffs of cigarettes.

A single cigarette will put this cleansing action of the lungs out of business for anywhere from one-half hour to two hours. In the chain smoker or even the two-pack-a-day smoker, the cleansing mechanism doesn't get a chance to revive until he is asleep. By morning he has to resort to the emergency measure of coughing to eliminate it. The normal secretion of mucus is stepped up at smoking time to counteract the drying effect of the hot smoke.

A bad feature of this accumulation of debris in the lungs is that its elimination even by coughing is very often not entirely accomplished. The clogged air passages in the tiny air sacs provide an excellent breeding ground for infection. At the same time, there occurs the continued irritation by chemicals in close, prolonged contact with living tissue, and the development of respiratory illness such as chronic bronchitis, emphysema, and lung cancer often follows. A contributing factor in this lung damage seems to be the constriction of the tiny capillaries in the air sacs caused by addiction to nicotine. This constriction prevents the blood from helping in the repair of damaged tissue.

Not too surprisingly, considering all the other harmful effects of the chemicals in tobacco smoke, a study by Dr. Harry Daniel, reported in the *Annals of Internal Medicine,* indicates that smokers are more likely to suffer from wrinkling of the skin than nonsmokers. The study conducted among 1,000 men and women focused upon the effects of smoking on the skin of the face. It revealed a greater prevalence of wrinkling among smokers, particularly in the development of crowsfeet and other wrinkles around the eyes.

Research has also proven what many nonsmokers have long suspected – smoking can be harmful to your eyes. Heavy smokers may be limiting their ability to see as well as they could, according to a leaflet published by the American Optometric Association. Nicotine and carbon monoxide in cigarette smoke are the main culprits in reducing night vision. Both can be involved in cutting the oxygen supply to the eyes, which can hinder adaption from dark to light. The finding that smokers tend to have a narrower field of view poses a hazard to drivers, who must be able to see "out of the corner of the eye." This faculty is needed to prevent accidents involving vehicles or persons approaching from the side of the road.

A less common condition is tobacco amblyopia, which leads to a loss of vision sharpness and color perception. It is often due to a combination of smoking, alcohol abuse, and poor diet and may improve when the individual stops smoking.

External eye irritation from cigarette smoke is perhaps the most common complaint of both smokers and nonsmokers. About 70 percent of people queried mentioned such irritation, which can be an extremely uncomfortable problem for people suffering from allergies and for contact lens wearers. Eye irritation, of course, is not the only problem that smoking causes for the nonsmokers. Evidence continues to grow showing effects on the nonsmoker similar to those encountered by the smoker, himself.

We have talked about the many illnesses and conditions caused by smoking, some relatively minor such as a nagging cough or reddened eyes and some much more serious. What can happen when a major smoking-related illness develops?

Art was the director of a health agency in a western city. He was married, had three children, and looked forward to the day when he could retire at a lake cabin he had purchased in Canada. He was a heavy smoker but wanted badly to quit, calling the habit stupid and dangerous. Numerous times he tried to kick the habit but was unsuccessful.

He continued to smoke year after year and finally developed cancer of the lung. Because Art had many friends who were physicians, he received the very best treatment that medical science could offer. One day after he had completed a series of difficult treatments, he said to a friend, "I think I've got this thing licked." That same day he served as chairman of a meeting, and he was in the best of spirits.

Just two weeks later, it was a different story. Art drove to a meeting at the state capital, about 100 miles from his home. Several times during the meeting, he was seized with spells of coughing and on one occasion had to leave the room. After the meeting, he said to a friend, "I wish I had known you were coming. I could have given you a ride. Driving up here alone gave me too much time to think."

For the next few weeks, Art did not come to work, although his secretary said again and again that he would be returning "any day now." Finally one afternoon he showed up at the office, but it was only for a couple of hours. Later, members of his staff sadly asked one another if they would ever see him again.

A few days later, he died at his home, just seven months after the lung cancer had been diagnosed.

Effects of Alcohol

An estimated 100 million Americans drink alcoholic beverages of one kind or another. Some are only occasional users, others are considered to be social drinkers who imbibe rather frequently. There are also alcohol abusers and outright alcoholics, the latter category making up about 10 percent of the drinking population. This means that in the United States, there are about 10 million alcoholics.

The effects of alcohol can be noticed almost immediately by the drinker, because alcohol doesn't have to be digested like food. Alcohol passes through the walls of the stomach and the small intestine directly into the blood, where it is carried to the brain. Some people have the idea that the more alcohol that is drunk the more stimulated the drinker will become. The truth is that any amount of alcohol acts as a central nervous system depressant. This effect impairs the ability of the brain to control various areas of the body.

The signs of drinking are all too well known and include a staggering gait, other uncoordinated movement, and slurred, thick speech. Although alcohol does not act directly upon the legs or the tongue, it depresses the portion of the brain responsible for walking and talking. After circulating through the brain, alcohol is carried to other parts of the body where it is broken down or metabolized into carbon dioxide and water. Most of this metabolic action is accomplished by the liver, although a small percentage of the alcohol is eliminated in the breath, the perspiration, the urine, and even the saliva.

About a half hour is needed by the body to process each half ounce of alcohol. A larger amount of alcohol, say the amount in four 16-ounce cans of beer, gives the liver several hours of work to get rid of the effects. If the individual goes on drinking more alcohol, the effects grow worse. Since the body is not given sufficient time to process the first drink, additional alcohol accumulates in the blood. This piling up of alcohol in the blood causes the individual to have successive behavior changes, finally resulting in drunkenness.

At 1 part alcohol per 2,000 parts of blood, a blood alcohol level of .05 percent, the drinker feels relaxed and carefree. In this condition, he may do or say something he would not even consider when perfectly sober. A youth or anyone else with this blood alcohol level might make an unfriendly gesture or a comment that could lead to an argument or even a fight.

A Navy petty officer who had been drinking in an enlisted men's club with some of his shipmates tried to start a fight with one of his friends, whom he accused of being a foreign spy. After the petty officer had sobered up and had been told about his actions, he was disgusted with himself. He sought out his friend and apologized for what he had done.

Two commissioned officers who had been drinking while on liberty in a West Coast port decided to swim to their ship anchored in the harbor about a mile from shore. Discarding their uniforms, they dived into the water, and after a long swim through high waves, the exhausted officers were dragged aboard by enlisted men on watch. Since neither of the officers was a good swimmer, they admitted later they would never have attempted the swim if they had been sober.

At a level of .10 percent, 1 part of alcohol to 1,000 parts of blood, walking and talking are affected. At .20 percent, the drinker wobbles about as he walks and might want to sleep or go on a crying jag. Impairment of the immune system of the body occurs at .25 percent. White cells in the blood can be reduced as much as those of a patient in severe shock. At .40 or .50 percent, the drinker lapses into a coma. The lower brain where breathing and heartbeat are controlled is affected by still higher levels of alcohol, and death can result.

Why do some people become silly drinking beer while others get sleepy? Why is it that some drinkers grow more friendly while others become nasty? The sailor we described turned ugly after drinking and made a foolish accusation about a friend. As the Blue Cross booklet *Alcoholism* points out, alcohol is a perplexing drug that still is not completely understood, and its effects can be different from one individual to another. It may even act differently on the same person from one time to another.

How you feel and act after drinking depends in part upon how much you drink and over what period of time. Effects depend not only upon how much a person drinks but also upon how fast the drinking is done, and other factors. The faster an individual drinks, the more the drug gets into and stays in the brain. The other factors that affect how someone feels and acts after drinking include how much the individual weighs. A 180-pounder has more blood and water in his body than does a 120-pound person. The same amount of alcohol will become diluted to a greater extent in the bloodstream of the heavier individual, and it will not affect him as quickly or as powerfully as it will affect the 120-pounder.

As the National Council on Alcoholism booklet Kids and Alcohol points out, how much experience the drinker has had with alcohol is another factor. People who have been consuming alcohol for many years have learned how they react to it. If they keep their drinking within certain limits, they exert considerable control over what they say and do while drinking. Yet another factor is how much the drinker has eaten. When people drink while they eat or soon after eating, the food in their stomachs makes it harder for the alcohol to get into the small intestine. Most alcohol goes into the bloodstream and then to the brain only after it reaches the small intestine.

When you drink alcohol, many of the organs in your body are affected either directly or indirectly. A number of health problems are related to drinking, including mental and emotional illness, heart disease, inflammation of the pancreas, irritation of the intestinal tract, bone marrow problems, low blood sugar, liver disease, and diseases of the bones and joints.

The alcoholic may develop delerium tremens when he tries to stop drinking. This condition is marked by tremors, hallucinations, and convulsions. The individual usually perspires profusely, has a rapid heart beat, enlargement of the pupils of the eyes, and fever. Death occurs in about one out of six individuals who develop delirium tremens. Other complications of chronic alcoholism may be mental confusion and apathy as well as inability to learn and a memory that deteriorates.

Alcohol produces changes in the circulation due to the dilitation of the blood vessels at the surface of the body. This interferes with maintaining body temperatures through the mechanism that regulates body heat. Congestion of blood in the skin brings about a feeling of warmth but leads to excessive heat loss. There is no increase of heat production in tissues, however, to make up for

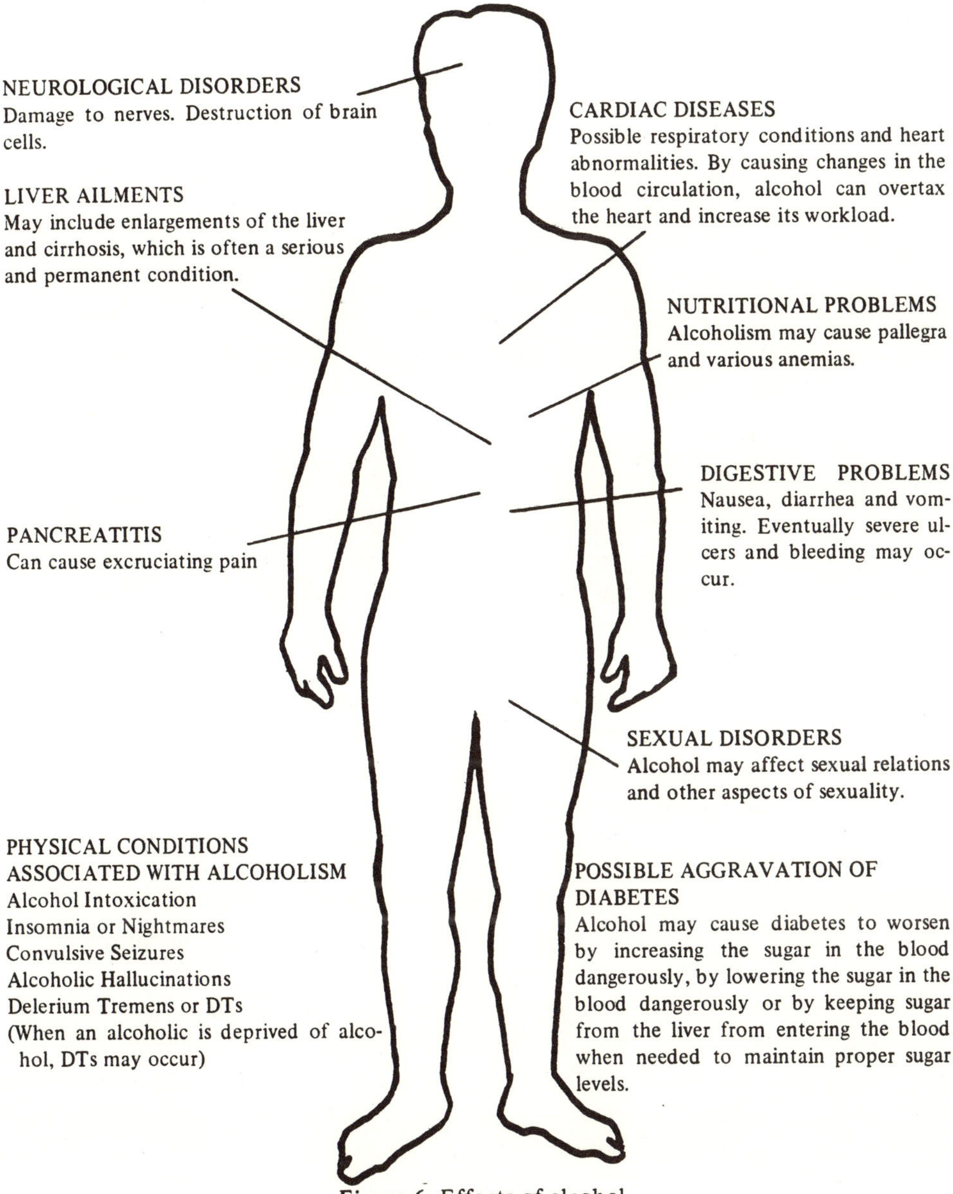

Figure 6. Effects of alcohol.

this loss. The individual feels warm, but the temperature deep in the body is lowered. During exposure to very cold weather, the effects of alcohol can be serious. Because of the depressant effect of alcohol on nerve tissue, the individual does not realize how cold he is, and responses to the brain are slowed. This explains why street people who have been drinking heavily to warm up on a cold night are sometimes found frozen to death in the morning.

Yet another complication of chronic alcoholism is muscle aching and tenderness and also severe weakness, which may prove to be permanent. Some investigators believe that unexplained heart failure in young and middle-aged adults is most often related to continued heavy drinking. These patients complain of fatigue, shortness of breath, heart irregularities or chest pain. If they go on drinking, the problem gets worse and develops into severe congestive heart failure.

Alcoholics often complain of long-lasting or acute intestinal problems including, vomiting, diarrhea, and loss of appetite. Eventually severe ulcers and hemorrhaging may result. Even more serious are the problems of pancreatitis and gastritis, which alcoholics often develop. It is believed that 20 to 40 percent of all patients with acute pancreatitis are heavy drinkers. Because of the severe pain of this illness, some of the victims become addicted to narcotics. Since alcoholic drinks may increase the secretion of gastric acid, stomach tissue may be damaged, leading to a widespread gastritis. In some of these patients, massive bleeding from the stomach may occur with all of the complications that such a situation involves.

The bone marrow function is affected by heavy consumption of alcohol. The chronic drinker may have anemia as well as changes in certain elements in the blood, even though he does not experience gastrointestinal bleeding. Changes in metabolism may take place in alcoholics, perhaps the most serious being alcoholic hypoglycemia, a pronounced drop in the blood sugar. This may be a factor in the sudden deaths that occur among alcoholics.

Although alcohol apparently does not cause diabetes or even contribute to its development, it may aggravate the condition of the diabetic by altering blood sugar levels and affecting the body's metabolism of sugar in general. It may also keep sugar from the liver from entering the blood when needed to maintain proper sugar levels. This is likely to happen when before-dinner cocktails are consumed and drinking is done on an empty stomach.

Of special concern to women are the effects of drinking by the expectant mother. Drinking during pregnancy can result in the altered growth and development of the infant. It is believed that even small amounts of alcohol can be a hazard to the fetus. This problem is discussed in Chapter 5.

As far as the public is concerned, perhaps the most commonly known complication of chronic drinking or alcoholism is liver disease. There are several forms of alcoholic liver disease, including fatty involvement of the liver, alcoholic hepatitis, and cirrhosis. Fat in the liver can be detected in two or three days following even moderate amounts of alcohol on a daily basis. All alcoholics and heavy drinkers show fatty involvement of the liver, a condition that may be linked with the more serious illnesses of the liver.

The most dreaded complication of chronic alcoholism in its effects upon the liver is cirrhosis which is found in some 8 to 10 percent of all chronic alcoholics. This condition is often accompanied by enlargement and bleeding and in some cases is fatal. Still another problem associated with alcoholism is alcoholic hepatitis, a condition accompanied by severe abdominal pain, fever, jaundice, and elevation of the white count in the blood.

The drinking of alcohol is clearly related to damage of a number of body organs. Alcoholics have a high death rate because of these complications. Further studies are needed to find out whether these complications also contribute to death and illness in social drinkers and others who consume alcohol in moderation and even in small amounts.

Effects of Other Drugs

Marijuana, often called pot, is among the most widely used of all of the drugs of abuse. Estimates have been made that more than 43 million Americans have tried pot. It is sometimes classified as a hallucinogen, sometimes as an intoxicant, and sometimes as a distinctive kind of drug is a category of its own.

Of the 43 million Americans who have tried pot, 16 to 20

million are regular users. Of this number, approximately 4 million are under 17 years of age. Furthermore, the age at which use begins is dropping and is now about 13 years. Depending upon any powerful substance such as alcohol or even coffee is a cause of worry for parents, teachers, and others who work with youth as well as for many youths themselves. Other aspects of marijuana use that are a reason for alarm is its growing use by teenagers and the appearance of more potent kinds of marijuana.

Marijuana comes from the cannabis plant, which grows wild or in cultivation in many parts of the world. One of the oldest of all drugs, marijuana is known by such names as "grass," "weed," "tea," "pot," and "Mary Jane." At one time used mainly by musicians, marijuana gained popularity among great numbers of people in the 1960s. Numerous musicians and artists who used marijuana felt it helped them to be more creative, but some of these same persons have now given up the drug because they believe it failed to live up to its reputation as a substance that improved creativity.

Certain doctors feel that cannabinoids, the chemical found only in the cannabis plant from which marijuana and hashish are prepared, have a broader cellular action on the body than any other drug of abuse. Only a few of the dozens of cannabinoids identified so far in marijuana have been studied. The truth is that cannabinoids make up only a fraction of the more than 400 known chemicals in the cannabis plant. In contrast, most drugs of abuse such as LSD, cocaine, and alcohol are single chemicals. Simply stated, this means marijuana's effects may very possibly prove to be more varied and extensive than almost any other drug of abuse.

If you are a user of pot, you should know that evidence is increasing that shows the drug has harmful effects on body functions, both physical and mental. Physically, the drug enters the bloodstream and acts on the brain and the nervous system. It is true that there is quite a bit of uncertainty about just how damaging pot really is, but it seems clear that there are powerful and complicated immediate effects, even though much remains to be learned about the long-range effects.

Marijuana affects mood, thinking, behavior, and judgement in

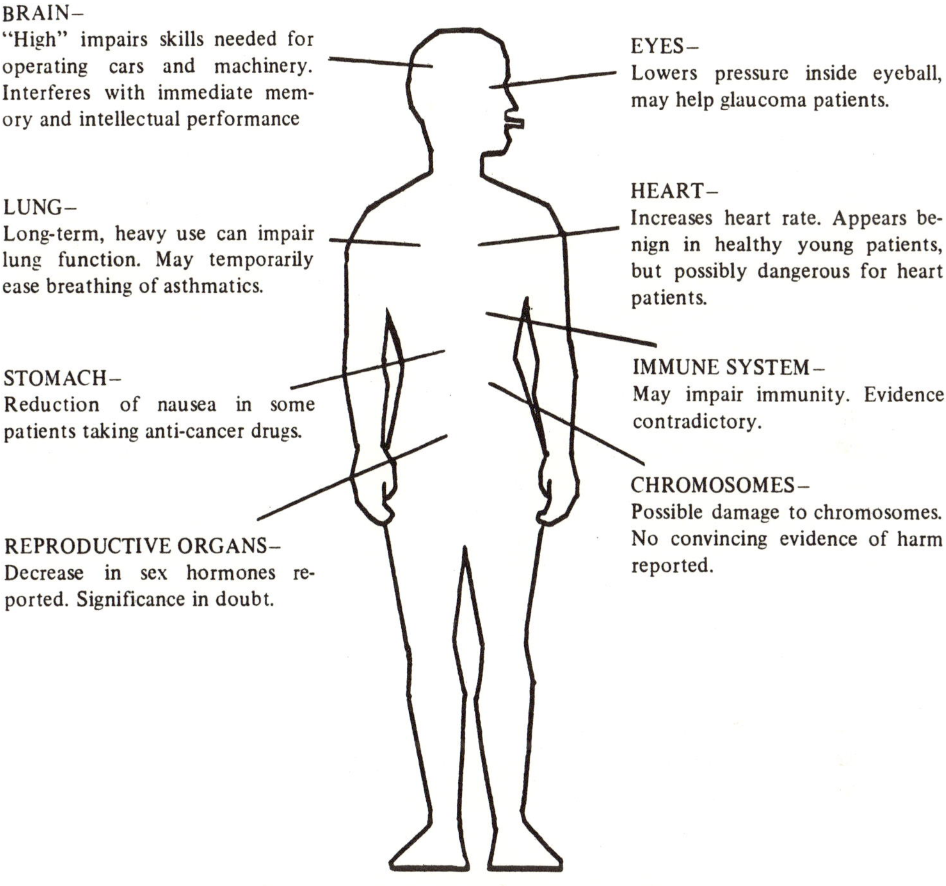

Figure 7. Effect of marijuana on the body.

a variety of ways. In large doses, it may result in hallucinations. One of the immediate effects is the psychological "high" for which pot has been noted for thousands of years. There is just no doubt that people high on marijuana suffer impaired skills needed for driving or for operating machinery such as a lathe. A marijuana user driving an automobile could easily lose control of the vehicle and smash into another car. Operating machinery such as an electric saw, hedge clipper, or power mower could result in a gashed wrist or a severed finger or toe. Admittedly, many youths stoned on marijuana are driving today or operating equipment and escaping injury, possibly because they are compensating for their impairment by using special caution.

The marijuana high also interferes with immediate memory and hinders reading comprehension, solving of arithmetic problems, and thinking in general. In these days of intense competition for scholarships and jobs, anything less than an individual's best effort can result in missed opportunities in education and a career.

Marijuana may also have harmful effects on the body's immune system. This is the capacity of the body to resist infectious agents such as germs and other foreign elements such as cancer cells. If this proves to be true, the pot user would be more likely to come down with certain infectious diseases as well as some chronic illnesses because of a decrease in the infection-fighting white cells in the blood.

Marijuana has a drastic effect upon the heart rate. Among youths who are stoned several hours every day, the heart rate is elevated from an average of 70 beats per minute to 130 or more. This could be the cause of heart pain experienced by youths who are chronic pot smokers. Speeding up of the heart rate may not be a serious matter among healthy individuals, but for anyone with a heart condition, the rapid rate could lead to a dangerous or even life-threatening situation. It was found that among heart patients who got 10 puffs of a marijuana cigarette, their heart rate jumped from 70 to 100.

Pot smokers face the same kind of damage to their respiratory tract as do tobacco smokers. As with tobacco, there are cancer-causing chemicals and numerous other poisonous substances in the tar of the marijuana smoke. Many of the immediate and long-range effects of smoking cigarettes are very likely similar to those of smoking pot and, in fact, may occur more quickly in pot users.

Studies in Germany among American soldiers showed that heavy cannabis smoking resulted in sinusitis, bronchitis, asthma, and other respiratory disorders in a year or less. This contrasts with the 10 to 20 years usually required for tobacco smoking to bring the same results. Certain carcinogens have, in fact, been found to be present in marijuana smoke in an amount 50 to 70 percent greater than in the smoke of tobacco cigarettes. Condensates of both marijuana and tobacco smoke painted on the backs of mice have produced cancerous tumors.

According to the book *Marijuana Today,* marijuana derivatives have an effect upon human genes and chromosomes, and the products of cannabis are absorbed into the ovaries and testes. On a television program that included physicians and health educators as participants, it was pointed out that very heavy use of marijuana – 8 to 16 joints per day – has been found drastically to lower the sperm count. Since many pot users are under 17 years of age, there could possibly be serious effects on future generations from pot use today. This is particularly true because pot use has been shown to change the morphology or size and shape of the sperm.

The television program brought out that sperm counts as low as 20 million per cubic centimeter (cc) of semen have been reported in at least one area of the nation. The concensus of the participants was that, in general, the sperm count is decreasing. The average sperm count has ordinarily ranged between 50 to 70 million per cubic centimeter of semen. Reasons for the decrease being noted today are believed to include toxic environmental agents, stress, and drugs.

A new threat to marijuana users has recently been reported in the *New England Journal of Medicine.* Fungus infections have been found in 50 percent of marijuana smokers in a study at the University of Wisconsin. These infections by the aspergillis fungus may lead to allergies or serious lung infections. The aspergillis fungus is the same type that grows in dark basement corners. It appears that pot smokers inhale the fungal spores into their lungs as they smoke. One of the pot smokers was found to be a "walking fungus ball" with fungus growing on his skin, lungs, nose, and kidneys. Dr. Steven Kagen, who reported the study, said he has yet to find a marijuana sample that does not contain fungal organisms. Because aspergillis fungi seem to retain their potency even in a burning joint, once they are inhaled, the organisms grow and may cause asthma, fever, and coughing. "Even if the smoker has no symptoms," Dr. Kagen said, "the organisms may invade and clog tiny branches of the lung. Eventually the blockage will impair the smoker's breathing."

Figure 8. A study at the University of Wisconsin found fungus infections in 50 percent of marijuana smokers.

The reason that there is aspergillis contamination in marijuana may be because pot is ordinarily smuggled into the United States in the hull of a ship or in airplane cargo bays, both of which are enclosed dark areas conducive to fungal growth.

The user of heroin, a narcotic derived from opium, must contend with a variety of health risks, both physical and emotional. Because heroin is usually taken by injection, the user faces the possibility of hepatitis and other infections, particularly from needles that have not been properly sterilized. Day after day of injecting into veins results in the veins becoming plugged with talcum powder, dirt, and other debris. Because veins lead to the heart, the infection of endocarditis is yet another threat.

The more frequently injecting is done, the more likelihood there is that the user will infect himself with any number of germs that are always present on skin, clothing, and syringe. There is always the special danger that the addict will contract hepatitis, a lengthy, weakening illness that causes jaundice or yellowing of the skin and eyes and may result in permanent damage to the liver. The liver serves as a storehouse of important substances for the body, and once it is seriously scarred, the damaged tissue may never be repaired. The heroin addict is often afflicted with skin rashes, ulcerating sores, and abscesses. Heavy use of drugs can lead to poor body hygiene and poor control of body functions such as incontinence – bedwetting at night and soiling of clothes during the day. One result may be severe constipation, which can only be relieved by such methods as continual use of certain drugs. Since addicts usually do not have the time, money, or inclination to get medical or dental attention, they learn to live with these problems and others such as infections of the teeth and gums. Because they often eat diets heavy in sweets, fail to brush their teeth regularly, and have other poor dental health practices, they often have widespread tooth decay, tooth loss, and gum illnesses such as periodontal disease. Poor eating and bad general health habits often give the addict a pale, hollow-eyed appearance.

As the addict continues to inject himself, at first in the arms and later in the legs, the more scarred his body will become and the more difficulty he will have in locating a spot where the hypodermic needle can be jabbed. Sticking a needle into a vein is not only a dangerous practice but also a painful one. Finally as veins collapse from repeated injections and arms and legs grow increasingly covered with small scars, he will search for any site where a vein can be injected. Eventually, in desperation, he will inject himself under the tongue or in the genitals.

Among the effects of heroin abuse are loss of judgement, loss of self-control, and decreasing appetite and weight. Heroin abusers are often described as being "on the nod." They drift into daydreaming, wake up, and drift off again. Mental deterioration often accompanies the chronic use of the drug. Withdrawal from heroin brings about symptoms similar to a severe case of influenza. Among the symptoms are nausea, cramps, chills, sweating, watery eyes, and a runny nose. Restlessness and sleeplessness are other signs of withdrawal, which can be a painful and sometimes dangerous process.

Since heroin is usually available only from illegal sources, control is lacking in both quality and potency. By the time the heroin reaches the street, the drug is usually diluted to less than 10 percent of its pure strength. The risk of a fatal dose is, however, always present, because the user can never be certain about the strength of the "bag" he purchases.

Barbiturates are depressants with wide medical uses such as sedating patients, relieving anxiety, and controlling high blood pressure, epilepsy, and chemically caused convulsions. When abused, barbiturates can be even more dangerous than heroin. Once the pattern of abuse develops, a physical and psychological dependence occurs, similar to that of heroin. Because these drugs severely distort judgement and the user is unable to keep track of how much he has taken, an overdose can easily follow.

Overdosing often results in slurred speech, drowsiness, staggering, and other appearances of being drunk. The individual may also show a violent temper and a quarrelsome disposition. Barbiturates are among the drugs most often identified as leading to accidental poisoning because no tolerance develops to a lethal dose. Withdrawal from barbiturates is especially dangerous since it can lead to severe discomfort and convulsions, which may be fatal. Deaths can result from either unsupervised withdrawal or an overdose.

Although tranquilizers are quite different from barbiturates, their effects are somewhat the same in terms of addiction and physical dependence. An example of a nonbarbiturate depressant also in the class of sedative hypnotics is methaqualone. High chronic use of any of these drugs can cause a barbituratelike dependence with similar hazards.

Just as barbiturates are frequently labeled "downers" because of their depressing effects upon the central nervous system, amphetamines are called "uppers" because they stimulate it. They are used in medicine for fatigue, certain kinds of mental depression, and in some instances for weight loss. In addition to their use in medicine, the amphetamines are used by truck drivers fighting to stay awake on long hauls, by students studying for examinations, by athletes getting ready for big games, and by housewives who feel they need more energy to carry out their housework, all of which represent misuse and can lead to addiction. The amphetamines can drive the user to exert himself beyond his physical capacities. Other effects are fatigue, dizziness, and feelings of fear and confusion. A dependence on amphetamines sometimes develops, which can bring about serious physical and mental problems. Withdrawal from amphetamines can lead to a suicidal depression.

One of the more common stimulants that is abused is methamphetamine, or speed. Although death seldom results from amphetamine abuse, there can be extensive psychological effects from heavy usage, including hyperactivity, mental confusion, and hallucinations.

Cocaine, a stimulant, is derived from the South American coca bush. Once employed as a local anesthetic, it now has no medical uses. It has been used off and on in the United States but recently has become one of the "in" drugs, and its popularity seems to be growing. Cocaine is such a powerful stimulant that it is sometimes taken in combination with depressants and in some cases even with heroin. The cocaine high may be followed by mental and physical depression. In heavy dosage, cocaine can cause heart and respiration functions to suffer such deep depression that death can follow. Although cocaine users do not become physically addicted, they can become mentally dependent. Initial stimulation from cocaine may be replaced by depression, restlessness, and weakness. Following continued use, side effects can consist of nausea, delirium, convulsions, fever, and diminished vision.

LSD is the best known of a series of hallucinogens that includes mescaline, psilocybin, DMT, PCP (Angel Dust), and some varieties of morning glory seeds. A resolution of the American Medical Association has this to say about hallucinogens: "These drugs can produce uncontrollable violence, overwhelming panic . . . or attempted suicide or homicide, and can result, among unstable individuals or those with preexisting neurosis or psychosis, in severe illness demanding protracted stays in mental hospitals."

The hallucinogens are extremely dangerous and unpredictable, especially for people using them for the first time. Mental effects have led to a number of accidental deaths, such as falls from windows, as well as suicide. Severe psychotic reactions can take place, some involving "flashbacks" occurring weeks or months after the drug was taken. Users have delusions of being invulnerable. Because normal judgements are distorted, there is danger of bodily injury to the user as well as to others.

Chemicals that can cause immediate and long-term harm to users are inhalants, such as solvents, aerosols, and anesthetics. Sometimes termed deliriants, they are defined as chemicals that give off fumes or vapors which, when inhaled, produce symptoms similar to intoxication. Results of using these substances include mental confusion, excitement, and hallucinations. Every household stores a number of products containing volatile solutions, often kept in cupboards, on shelves, under sinks, and in other areas easily reached by children. These products include gasoline, lighter fluid, airplane and household cements, nail polish remover, paint thinners, and kerosene. Aerosol containers are used to package a variety of products such as deodorants, hairsprays, and insecticides, many of which contain chlorinated or fluoridated hydrocarbons.

Inhaling the poisonous fumes from these substances, never intended to be breathed, can cause damage to the brain, lungs, spinal cord, and liver and in some cases can result in blindness and even death. Use of a plastic bag held against the mouth to enhance the effects of these chemicals can cause death by suffocation. Most of the users of inhalants are youths between 10 and 15 years of age. These children usually have histories of family problems and failure in school and often live in economically deprived neighborhoods.

In concluding this chapter, we should like to pass along to you some information provided by the Do It Now Foundation, an organization concerned with giving you the facts about drug abuse. According to the Foundation, there are lots of street drugs going around including acid, speed, mescaline, reds, psilocybin, THC, and cocaine.

"You've probably heard about these already, and you probably know what most of them are supposed to do," the Foundation states. "But what you probably haven't heard is that many of them are impure, contain harmful adulterants, or are completely phoney."

Serious as the situation is in regard to the general effects of drugs we have described, the fact that many street drugs are impure, include adulterants, and just are not what they are claimed to be makes things even more hazardous for today's drug abuser.

Effects of drugs in terms of *COMMON SIGNS OF DRUG ABUSE* are listed beginning on page 165.

Chapter 4

CHANGES IN LIFE-STYLE AND OTHER DRUG EFFECTS

RECENT headlines across the country have stated that Americans are healthier today and taking better care of themselves than ever before. American's life expectancy at birth has continued to rise, with women living 77 years and men almost 70, an increase from the 74 years for women and 67 years for men just a decade ago.

"The level of health in this country is good and getting better," Dr. Edward J. Brandt, Jr., Assistant Secretary of Health, said late in 1981 in presenting a report on the nation's health.

What are some of the factors that are contributing to the improved health of Americans? More than 30 million Americans, including 100,000 physicians, have quit smoking. Growing numbers of citizens are changing to a life-style that includes regular exercise and better eating habits. Swimming, jogging, hiking, bicycling, skiing, and working out at health spas or gymnasiums are becoming vital parts of people's lives. Also helping to improve the general health of the nation is that more and more people in their efforts to protect themselves against heart disease, stroke, and other illnesses are having their blood pressure checked periodically at their doctors' offices or in community screening programs sponsored by such agencies as the American Heart Association. Many individuals are having more frequent health checkups as part of a healthier life-style.

Al Meltzer, a well-known Philadelphia sports commentator, recently predicted that as the decade of the 1980s unfolds, we will see an unprecedented increase in nonspectator sports. People are getting a little tired of sitting around watching others perform,

Figure 9. Participation in activities such as tennis, golf, swimming, and jogging is a part of a more active life for many Americans.

Mr. Meltzer said. They will be spending less time engaged in such pastimes as playing cards, watching television, and listening to the radio and more time on the tennis and handball courts, at the swimming pool and the golf course. He forsees a tremendous increase in the use of all kinds of athletic equipment people can enjoy in their own backyards and on neighborhood courts, rinks, and playgrounds.

Buttressing Mr. Meltzer's observations is another trend. For many years, good health was considered as just being free from illness. Now, however, the term optimum health is being used, meaning the best possible health that an individual can have, and this is the goal for which each person should strive. A number of organizations including many local hospitals are not only conducting wellness programs for their own employees but are also reaching out into the community with their wellness activities.

There's yet another angle to the nation's eagerness to improve health and develop healthful life-styles. People are showing greater concern about the environment in which they live, work, and play. This is being reflected in the increasing nonsmokers rights movements promoted by such organizations as Group Against Smokers Pollution (GASP) and the National Interagency Council on Smoking and Health. A Nonsmokers Bill of Rights developed by the Council states that the smoker has no right to pollute the atmosphere that we all must breathe and that the rights of the nonsmoker supersede the rights of the smoker. Consequently, this means that the smoking interests and individual smokers will be pushed further into a corner much like a tired boxer who in the late rounds of a bout finds punches being thrown at him from all sides.

On the drinking front, groups such as Mothers Against Drunk Drivers (MADD) are demanding action to protect the public against the driver who is under the influence of alcohol. President Reagan has set up a national commission to study the problem of drinking and driving, and in Pennsylvania, Governor Dick Thornburgh organized a similar task force at the state level. Other states are almost certain to follow suit in organizing communities to find better ways of dealing with drinking and driving.

There is also increasing public sentiment against drug abuse as neighborhood groups unite to combat drugs. Some communities have gone so far as to combine their resources to keep methadone clinics and other treatment centers out of their areas. People argue that they don't want their children or themselves brought into contact with abusers and pushers, even though governmental and private agencies stress the need for such treatment programs.

In view of the trend in America today toward a healthier life-style that stresses health care rather than medical care, and greater concern for the environment, what is the outlook for the individual who abuses drugs? The self-defeating and dangerous life-style of the drug abuser affords a sharp contrast to the self-fulfilling and healthy life-style of many Americans noted by Secretary Brandt. There is just no way that the chronic drug abuser, the problem drinker, and the heavy smoker fit into the more active life-style that Al Meltzer envisions and that many citizens are, in fact, already enjoying.

Because we are talking about life-style, let's take a minute to define it. For our purposes, life-style involves all aspects of a person's life that in any way influence how he lives. One factor is physical status. An individual with physical problems is bound to have a different life-style than one who enjoys perfect health. Other aspects are social, intellectual/educational, emotional, and spiritual. All of these aspects have an impact upon how a person sets priorities, what he does for recreation and entertainment, how he selects friends, his philosophy of life, his self-concept, his sense of responsibility, and his habits, good and bad.

Drug abuse, whether limited or extensive, is certain to have an effect upon life-style. Unfortunately, some people still feel compelled to abuse dugs as a way of life, a way to shut out the real world, or seek a world of unreality. Others, youths in particular, have the idea that drug abuse is an adventure – a road to supposedly new and wonderful experiences. But what is the life of the person who is deeply into drugs really like? It is truly the exciting existence that some portray it to be?

Take the case of the heroin abuser, since heroin is a widely used drug and its use is even on the increase in some communities. The many physical effects of heroin abuse are described in Chapter 3. Heroin can be so addictive, both physically and psychologically, that a person, once he is hooked, thinks of little else. For him, heroin becomes a way of life his new life-style.

Several times during the day, the heroin abuser will dissolve some heroin powder on a spoon, draw it into a hypodermic syringe through a piece of cotton, which acts as a filter, and stab it into a vein. Reaction to the dose usually increases in relation to the amount of the dose. Repeated use results in increasing tolerance – the user must administer larger and larger doses to get the desired effect. This reinforces the compulsive behavior, known as drug addiction. The last thoughts of the drug abuser each night are to make certain that he has a supply for the next day. If not, he must somehow beg, borrow, or steal some. In many cases, this really means robbing someone, breaking into a house and stealing, or shoplifting articles that can be pawned or sold.

A study of drug addicts in Baltimore revealed that they committed six times more crimes when dependent on drugs that when off drugs. Dr. John Ball, professor of sociology at Temple University, codirector of the study, said that the average addict committed 2,000 offenses in the 11-year study period. Some committed no crimes, but one individual in the study was involved in almost 9,500 crimes, an average of more than two crimes a day. Theft was found to be the main type of crime. Addicts were also involved in drug sales and con games, however. Some of the addicts admitted that they robbed six or eight stores almost every day.

Other methods than crime are often used by addicts to obtain money for drugs. One 17-year-old girl who became addicted to heroin was adamant about not getting into crime to keep up her habit. Instead she worked at several jobs, taking on both day and night shifts. "If I could have been motivated to work that hard for some reason other than drugs, I could be on easy street, today," she commented. She finally turned to a methadone maintenance program in an effort to break her addiction.

As far as social aspects of living are concerned, the heroin addict must get along without recreational and entertainment activities most of us take for granted, since the addict's time is spent in dealing with a craving that must be satisfied 24 hours a day. Dr. Stephen Pittel points out that in the transition from one life-style to another, problems are sure to come up. The individual who makes the change from his usual life-style to the world of addiction has to learn that he will miss out on many enjoyments such as recreational pursuits he formerly had. Dr. Pittel, who is director of the Pacific Institute for Research and Evaluation at

Berkeley., says that the addict faces many of the same problems that confront the poor, the unskilled, and the ex-convict.

The addict must often scrape together whatever money he can accumulate to continue his habit. Costs of maintaining the heroin habit can be devastating, since they can amount to well over $100 a day. This means that $50,000 a year or more must somehow be furnished for the addiction alone, not to mention the many other expenses of day-to-day living. It is not at all surprising that to support the heroin habit the addict may have to turn to crimes such as robbery, shoplifting, forgery, and prostitution. Because intended victims may resist, the addict can find himself involved in an assault or a murder he had no intention of committing when he started on his crime spree.

Carl Eller, the former Minnesota Viking All-Pro, found that the cocaine habit was even more expensive. Finding that alcoholic highs weren't enough, he went on to freebasing cocaine, a habit that cost him $1,000 a day. He spend every cent he had on the drug, using all the money he had saved to open a business after his football career. He was so deeply into the drug that he pawned his three National Football Conference rings. "Basing is self-defeating," he told the *Sporting News.*

> You have frustrations and anxieties when you come down from that quick high. You want to recapture the feeling right away, so you have to go up again. That's when it starts to get expensive.
>
> By this time, you really are cut off from reality. You don't know what's going on in life. You believe you can do everything. You really can't do anything.
>
> If you choose that rush, the rest of the world passes you by. And you develop extreme paranoia . . . paranoia like you wouldn't believe.

The addict must often be sneaky, secretive, and manipulative not only with family and friends but also with people from whom he hopes to get drugs. Because he spends so much time on his habit, he has little time left to work at his job or, if he loses one job, to look for another. In addition, if he is a youth, he frequently has not learned a trade or gotten into a profession, so he is unable to qualify for many positions. Like the poor, he may not have enough money to eat well-balanced meals, which often affects his health and appearance. In one Italian city, the drug addicts who turn up in the city's plaza at night are referred to as "emaciated waifs."

Changes in appearance for the worse have a harmful effect on life-style. Self-concept is influenced, causing loss of confidence and withdrawal. One young addict who was a musician found that when she looked in the mirror in the morning, she saw reflected a person with sallow skin, pimples, rashes, and a scrawny body. She asked herself how she could get off the habit. Yet, she was too weak and apathetic to do anything about breaking it. Addicts, in fact, often develop certain characteristics such as peculiar mannerisms, unusual facial expressions, and a strange appearance in and around the eyes. Addicts looking out over a crowd of people can often recognize other addicts almost instantly.

Although they make new friends and acquaintances through their addiction, addicts will frequently find that old friendships of long standing break up. One of the reasons is that addicts must have contacts who can help them gain access to drugs, something that former friends usually cannot do. Another reason is that old friends cannot bear to see addicts go downhill physically and emotionally and will do everything in their power to help. Because addicts may not want assistance, their refusal may be the final act that ends friendship.

Still another reason why old friendships fail to survive is that heavy drug users and addicts often have physical impairments. They may no longer have the energy to dance, ski, skate, and take part in other activities they formerly found appealing and around which friendships were built.

To keep up with his habit, the addicted person must have information about local sources of drugs. For the ghetto addict this often means walking around dangerous rundown neighborhoods and associating with pimps, prostitutes, and pushers. Because most of the money he accumulates goes to sustain his habit, an addict sometimes must live in bad neighborhoods in poorly heated rooms with broken plumbing and infestations of rats and insects.

Because drug addicts are no longer in control of their lives, they exist for years on the edges of society, only half alive, half free. Over months or years, addicts lose interest in school, in careers, in family. They have few friends who are not also on drugs. Because they have neither the time nor the energy to keep up social contacts, their only purpose in life becomes the search for enough drugs to keep "high" and avoid the agony of sudden drug deprivation.

Drug addiction leads to changes in the priorities a person sets for himself. When family and job are no longer top priorities and the number one priority becomes drugs, changes in life-style are certain to take place. Don Reese, a defensive end with the New Orleans Saints in the 1981 football season, had a drug habit that lasted for several years. He said that cocaine "has dominated my life one way or another almost every minute," since he was picked by the Miami Dolphins as its first round draft choice in the 1974 college draft. He said that the drug took control of his life and almost killed him. Even as late as mid-1982, he was still being plagued by problems caused by his former drug habit.

Addicts may turn themselves in voluntarily for treatment when they realize that they have little hope of overcoming the dismal condition in which they find themselves. Giving up an addiction is not simple, however. Some states have compulsory commitment – addicts are sent to hospitals rather than prison when they are arrested for possession of drugs. Under federal law, persons who are addicts and who are charged with or convicted of any federal offense can be committed for treatment. Addicts not charged with any offense may possibly be committed if they seek treatment.

Withdrawing from heroin and the benzodiazepines can be a painful process. The extent of physical symptoms that occurs is related to the amount of the drug dose used daily. Depriving the body of an addictive drug causes excitability of those same bodily functions that were depressed by the use of the drug. With deprivation of the drug, withdrawal symptoms usually show up shortly before the next dose is due. Complaints, pleas, and demands by the addict for the drug grow more frequent as time elapses and the body is deprived of the drug following the metabolism of the last dose.

Symptoms of narcotics withdrawal include watery eyes, runny nose, yawning, sweating, restlessness, irritability, loss of appetite, sleeplessness, goose flesh, tremors, and severe sneezing. The patient is weak and depressed, and stomach cramps and diarrhea often appear. Heart rate and blood pressure climb, and there may be chills with flushing or reddening of the skin and heavy perspiration.

Still other signs may be pain in the bones and muscles of the back and arms and legs as well as muscle spasms. Kicking movements that develop may well be the source of the expression "kicking the habit." At this point, the patient may become suicidal. Without treatment, the withdrawal eventually runs its course in seven to ten days. When the individual will return to normal cannot be predicted. For several weeks after withdrawal, the individual will continue to brood about his drug use and will be likely to succumb to any temptation to use drugs again. Even such things as the sight of a building similar to one in which drugs were taken or an odor reminiscent of drug taking may rekindle the person's use of drugs. Or the individual may visit friends who take drugs to have coffee with them or smoke cigarettes and will be under great temptation to return to drug use.

Another hazard of the use of narcotic drugs is overdosing. Since there is no easy way to determine the purity of a drug sold on the street, the potency cannot be guaranteed. A person with a mild overdose may be stuporous or asleep. Coma may result from larger doses. Among symptoms are slow, shallow breathing and clammy, cold skin. The body grows limp and the jaw relaxes. There is a danger that the tongue may fall back, blocking the air passageways. In severe cases, there may be convulsions followed by respiratory arrest and death. Hospitals are equipped with special equipment and antidotes for narcotic poisoning.

Difficult as withdrawal may be, it is often harder to keep from backsliding once withdrawal is completed. In trying to stay off narcotics, the addict must overcome strong underlying needs to take the drugs. The help of doctors and social workers as well as hospitals and social service agencies is often required to rehabilitate the narcotic abuser so that he can return to a drug-free life-style.

So far, we have talked about drugs producing physical dependence. Much of what has been stated has parallels with other drugs. A university student who was a heavy user of marijuana was asked to talk to a health class about his habit. He freely admitted that since he had started to smoke pot, his life-style had been altered. For one thing, he no longer enjoyed going home to visit his family, who lived about 150 miles from the campus. When he did go home, he tried to hide his pot smoking, because his family was opposed to any kind of drugs. As a result he often spent weekends hanging around his dormitory, and with time on his hands, he indulged in more pot smoking. This led to a continuing cycle in which he was soon entrapped.

He spent less time studying and concentrating on his homework. His grades dropped from Bs to Cs and Ds. He said he was no longer as friendly with certain people as he had been, and these included the "cop on the corner," with whom he had frequent conversations. In short, he said he had become less enthusiastic and studious, and as he became more discouraged about his efforts at school, he spent more time smoking pot. He regretted these changes in his life, although they still were not important enough to motivate him to quit smoking marijuana.

Studies by the Institute of Medicine of the National Academy of Sciences show that marijuana hampers short-term memory, impairs oral communications, slows learning, and may cause temporary periods of confusion, anxiety, and even delirium. All of these effects can be detrimental to life-style, particularly that of the high school or college student.

A habit similar to and closely related to smoking of marijuana is the smoking of tobacco, which also has powerful effects on life-style that are rarely appreciated. In the book *Learning to Live Without Cigarettes*, the authors point out the effects of cigarette smoking:

> Countless thousands of smokers have permitted cigarettes to dominate their lives. Their daily existance has become so cigarette-centered that all of their waking hours are regulated by the cigarette habit. A cigarette on awaking, one before breakfast, one with coffee, one after coffee, one waiting for the subway, one getting out of the subway, etc., etc., etc., etc. A daily ritual, strictly adherred to, without

deviation. No wonder, the housewife, off cigarettes for two weeks and nervous as a cat, answered when asked the time of day by her husband, "It's two cigarettes after eight."

The authors suggest that the smoker consider the cost of smoking and effect on his life-style – "in the loss of his self respect in that he finds himself dictated to be a three-inch cylinder of shredded tobacco. It is strange that in this country where we pride ourselves so much on our determination not to let ourselves be pushed around, we submit so meekly to the dictates of the tobacco leaf."

Many studies have attempted to correlate the smoking habit with various personality traits evident in an individual's life-style. Among these studies was a large British survey which found that smokers are greater risk takers, more impulsive, more prone to divorce and changes in job, more interested in sex, and more likely to drink tea, coffee, and alcohol.

Nicotine from an inhaled cigarette reaches the brain in seven seconds, twice as fast as from an intravenous injection. A pack-a-day smoker takes more than 70,000 puffs a year, a frequency of "shots" unmatched by any other drug taking. This frequency overwhelmingly involves the smoker in the habit.

As we have pointed out, the life-style of the smoker revolves around cigarettes. A teacher firmly believed and often commented that the only thing that helped him to get through the day was the friendly, between-class cigarette that gave him the needed lift to survive the next 35-minute bout with a class of lively teens. It never occurred to him that during his vacations in Canada, while basking in the summer sun, fishing, and relaxing, he continued to smoke his daily quota of cigarettes even though free of the frustrations of the job that always seemed to justify his smoking habit. In fact, he always made sure to supply himself in advance with 10 cartons of his favorite brands to carry him over the summer.

According to Dr. William Pollin, director of the National Institute of Drug Abuse (NIDA), cigarette smoking is the most widespread example of drug dependence in the country. He said that only an estimated 10 percent of people in the United States who use alcohol lose control of their level of use. The opposite is true of tobacco smokers, most of whom would like to cut down on their smoking or quit entirely. Many find it very difficult or impossible to do so.

"Nicotine is a psychoactive drug. It influences one's subjective state and behavior." Dr. Pollin added. "A major finding of current NIDA studies is the marked similarity that exists between morphine, cocaine, and nicotine."

Smokers and users of other drugs sometimes have a life-style that shows a lack of responsibility for themselves and other people. One woman who is an avid nonsmoker recently entertained three relatives, all of whom are heavy smokers. Even though they were well aware of their hostess's feelings about smoking, they smoked incessantly in her presence, failed to use ashtrays, and littered the house with cigarette butts, matches, and ashes.

Nonsmokers such as this woman are being subjected by smokers to far greater risks than previously believed, the Canadian Health Department warns. The Department states that one study of nonsmokers in a working environment demonstrated that passive smoking, the inhalation by nonsmokers of tobacco-polluted air, was equivalent to smoking 10 cigarettes a day.

The worst danger is not smoke exhaled by smokers, since their lungs and cigarette filters trap some of the worst pollutants, but sidestream smoke, the smoke that goes directly into the air from a burning cigarette. The major contribution to indoor pollution by tobacco smoking is the sidestream smoke, which contains NDMA, one of the most potent carcinogens known. The concentration of NDMA in sidestream smoke is 50 times greater than in mainstream or exhaled smoke.

Minute radioactive particles in cigarette smoke, already linked to lung cancer, may also be the source of malignant tumors throughout the bodies of heavy smokers, researchers reported in July 1982. The radioactive material collected in the mucous lining of the bronchial tubes is passed from the lungs throughout the entire body, Dr. R. T. Ravenholt of the federal Centers for Disease Control wrote in a letter published in the *New England Journal of Medicine.*

His letter was written in response to previous research findings reported in the journal, which stated that a one and one-half pack a day smoker received yearly doses of alpha radiation equal to 300 chest x-rays. Cigarette smoke results in radiation exposure to smokers and probably to nonsmokers regularly exposed to the smoking of others, the report stated. It appears that smokers are not only endangering their own life-style, but are also posing hazards that can affect the life-style of nonsmokers.

Alcohol is yet another drug that can seriously affect the life-style of the drinker himself as well as others. Alcohol consumption greatly influences the life-style of the problem drinker and increases susceptibility to infections, anemia, and diseases of the liver, heart, brain, and other organs. The heavy drinker is also more susceptible to cancer of the head and neck. Damage to the brain may make it necessary for the individual to be placed in an institution. Of all male admissions to state mental hospitals, 40 percent suffer from alcoholism.

Perhaps more than any other addiction, alcoholism affects the life-style of family members. Alcoholism has, in fact, aptly been termed "the family disease." Every member of the family is influenced by it, and the life-style of family members can be altered emotionally, spiritually, and in many cases economically, socially, and physically. Recent research cites similar findings and conclusions regarding the effect on the family of persons addicted to other drugs.

Each family member has a role he or she is expected to perform, and the behavior of each person has an effect upon others in the family. When alcoholism becomes established in family life, it can generate great power in shaping the life-style of the family. The very presence or absence of alcohol can be a vital factor in how family members react to one another. Alcoholism can become a force that moulds and reshapes the roles family members play, as individuals and as members of the family as a whole.

As Dr. Ruth Fox points out in the publication *Effect of Alcoholism on Children*, the child in the home affected by alcoholism has trouble in developing the trust and confidence needed for successful living. Unless each family member plays his or her role of mother, father, and child properly, the required examples are lacking for the child and his own self-image may become distorted.

Much of the material in the remainder of this chapter is based upon her publication.

For as long as she can manage it, the mother usually shelters the young child from the knowledge that his or her father is an alcoholic. Because of his drinking, the father may be late to family meals and other gatherings, or he may miss them completely. He may return home in the early morning hours after a drinking bout, or he may be absent from the home for several days.

When the young child finally learns of the problem, it is a shattering experience. It may be that he or she suspected the problem, but the stark realization is hard to bear. The child is then torn between loyalty to the father and love for him and revulsion over his actions. When sober, the alcoholic father is often charming, affectionate, understanding, and quick to forgive shortcomings in others, because he is so aware of his own. He inspires the natural love of his offspring, who tries to develop an image of the ideal father.

With the occurrence of other drinking bouts, the child faces growing disappointment. He/she becomes frustrated, finding that many of the normal activities such as shared family jokes and outings are denied. He/she may soon be lying awake at night listening for the rattle of keys in the lock, the sound of stumbling footsteps on the stairway, and the clamor of arguments between father and mother. The child may even blame him/herself for a drinking episode and feel that some shortcoming of his/her own may have triggered it. Instead of having the carefree, pleasant life-style of most of his/her peers, the child suffers harmful effects upon many aspects of his/her life.

As Ruth Fox points out, the daughter of a drinking father may face special problems. Instead of being the target of the father's hostility, he may show a seductive preference for her. This binds her closely to him so that she sides with him against the mother. However, since she is basically dependent upon the mother, she feels guilt and confusion. Believing that she is the only one with any influence over him, she may feel responsible when he drinks. She may also confuse masculine independence with drunkenness. These may be factors in the development of alcoholism later in her life.

There may also be traumatic effects upon others. Older youths in the family, male in particular, often spend hours worrying about the whereabouts of the father who has disappeared from the home and more hours searching for him in bars, hotels, and alleyways. If and when they find him, still more time is spent in trying to get him in condition so that he can return to home or job.

As the father's drinking further alienates him from the family, the mother will try to fulfill the roles of both mother and father. Some wives in their frustration will divorce their husbands. Understandably, the divorce rate is four times as high among alcoholics. Other wives will try to contend with almost any situation to keep the family together. This is especially true when marriage partners have been together for many years, and the wife pledges herself to hanging on for the remaining years, regardless of what happens.

Among reasons why the wife will endure the many problems of the marriage are that she believes alcoholism is a disease, and she refuses to forsake a person who is ill. Because of shame, fear of ridicule, and humiliation, the family will often try to stick together, but at the expense of having a happy life-style. Because children in the home fail to find the warmth, support, and example of a strong male model, they may join the "wrong gang" and become delinquent. Or they may spend most of their time within the family, giving up most of their outside contacts with friends.

Even children who have married and left the immediate family circle where there is an alcoholic father may find that their life-style is affected by what happens in the home of the parents. One young married man dreaded to get telephone calls from his mother which he received several times a month, usually on weekends -- "Dad is on a binge again. Please go look for him. He hasn't been home since night before last."

One middle-aged man who was kindly, gracious, and a good wage earner as an executive became domineering, cruel, and depraved when drunk. He beat his wife and abused his children. Three of the four children in the home were able to withstand the father's abusive tactics without suffering lasting harm to their personalities. However, the oldest son was seriously affected. He fell behind in his class at school where he was often in trouble because of his poor grades and his bad behavior. Known for his ability in sports, his play became inconsistent. When he finally graduated from high school, he was unable to find work and began to drink. He married but was soon separated from his wife and family. Jailed from time to time for drunkenness, he spent months driving aimlessly around the country in an old car heaped with his personal belongings.

The circumstances are different if the mother is an alcoholic. Because of her sheltered position in the home with no time sheets to sign and reports to turn in, she may begin to drink small amounts of alcohol. As she increases her drinking, she may become dependent upon it without the knowledge of the family. When questioned by the father, who eventually becomes suspicious, she may say that she needs an occasional drink to help her deal with the many household responsibilities. Eventually, because of the role that the mother plays in managing the home and in many cases disciplining the children, the life-style of the entire family will be influenced.

Often not knowing where to turn for help, the father may take no action for weeks or months, and when he finally does, the situation may be out of control. Because men are sometimes less patient than women in such instances, the father may abandon the family.

The alcoholic mother who has a very young child may be overly concerned about his care, or she may neglect him when he cries because he is wet or hungry. She may not feed the child at all, give him unappetizing food, or slap him when he refuses to eat what she has prepared. Infants can be greatly upset when they are neglected or hear arguments and may suffer skin rashes and diarrhea as a result.

Older children in the family may hesitate to bring their friends into the home. They may fear that the mother will be overly sentimental, or may be ill, stagger about, drop lighted cigarettes, break dishes or furniture, or fall down. They may refuse to go out to play because they are afraid that the mother may hurt herself. As a result they may fail to make the team or lose out on a part in the school play. The mother's hangover, with its physical illness, its remorse, its humiliation, its fears and anxieties can also be very painful to the children. They may fail to develop a stable personality, or they may feel that they come from a mother who is no good and that they can never amount to anything. Youths in such a situation may begin to drink as an escape from an environment that is making life intolerable.

Most of the 10 million alcoholics in the United States are employed and living in a family setting. Long before the employer suspects alcoholism, the family has been deeply involved in the problem with serious effects on both wife and children. In the case of the alcoholic husband, all kinds of efforts may be made by the family, particularly the wife, to deal with the problem and, if possible, to hide it. These include refusing invitations to social events and cutting down or even eliminating gatherings of friends in the home. Other efforts may consist of lying about how much drinking is being done, withholding of money or sex, calling in the police, or trying to arrange for commitment, separation, or divorce.

Victims of alcoholism are deeply affected on the job because of their disease. Absenteeism, wasted time and materials, missed appointments, accidents, and faulty decisions costing hundreds or even thousands of dollars are all common failings of employed alcoholics. One older man who had been a trusted employee of a company for 30 years and who had become an alcoholic agonized over wrong decisions he imagined he made during blackouts from his drinking while on the job. In most cases, the wrong decisions were imagined rather than real.

In the early stages of alcoholism, the employed alcoholic may be able to keep from drinking during long periods, particularly during working hours and in emergencies. In this way, his problem can be hidden from his boss and his co-workers and will be known only to his family. As the addiction grows worse and each binge is accompanied by a craving for more alcohol, he will continue to drink, disregarding his health, his business, his family, or any standards he may have set for himself.

Because he finally reaches the point where he cannot face life without alcohol, he develops alibis and defenses that keep him from admitting that he is addicted. Because social drinking plays such an important role in our culture, the alcoholic argues that his drinking is no different from that of other people. He may say that he is in control of his life and is not in need of help. Finally, however, his drinking becomes known to his boss and fellow workers, some of whom may try to help hide the difficulty. Eventually, the employer finds he must take some kind of action. This may consist of advice, referral for help, threats, or outright firing.

The alcoholic father described earlier had a long history of demotions, firings, rehirings, and promotions. When he was able to stay sober for long periods, his ability as an executive enabled him to support his family in elegant style. During such times, his family would live in a large colonial-style house in a fashionable suburb. A year or two later, they would abruptly move to an apartment or small house in the city as he would again succumb to his alcoholism.

Whether man or woman, the alcoholic may have changes in behavior, dress, and personality as his illness progresses. One young man who worked in business and industry and who was known for his fine appearance completely changed his life-style when he became an alcoholic. He slept wherever he could find shelter – in flop houses, curled up in a doorway, or on a newsstand in a subway concourse. One night he slept in one of his favorite spots – behind a billboard in a downtown section. When he awakened, he found that he was wearing worn, mismatched shoes and soiled stockings. He threw away the shoes and stockings and walked barefoot along a main street toward an alcohol rehabilitation center he had been to before. Carrying a bottle of witch hazel from which he took an occasional swallow, his only thought was to find a decent place to sleep that night.

Fortunately for him, he stayed at the rehabilitation center for treatment and today as a recovered alcoholic helps to counsel others addicted to alcohol.

Youths who drink heavily and who may well be on the road to becoming alcoholics often develop a life-style consisting of activities that make them look foolish in the eyes of their friends. These actions include boisterousness, arguing, fighting, and getting sick and throwing up. Such things are not considered "cool" by their friends and acquaintances, and youths who behave in these ways risk being snubbed by boys and girls whose friendship they value.

Addiction to drugs, alcohol, or tobacco never improves lifestyle. Becoming dependent upon any drug can only make lifestyle worse.

Chapter 5

FETAL ALCOHOL SYNDROME – WHAT IT DOES TO CHILDREN

MAUREEN was 28 years old and was expecting her first baby. Like other expectant mothers, she was happy and excited about the prospect of having a baby, but she also had a few worries. Could she and her husband afford the baby? Would it be a difficult birth? Could she handle the responsibility of caring for another person for 18 years or more? Perhaps the most frightening thought was this – will the baby be a normal, healthy child? Or will it be born with some kind of a physical or mental problem?

Maureen had always been quite a heavy drinker, and she continued to drink during her pregnancy. The baby was due in May, but Maureen went into labor the last week in April, and the baby, a boy, was born a few days early. When Maureen first saw the baby, she didn't quite know what to think or say. His eyes seemed very small, his nose was short and upturned, and he had an unusual amount of dark hair, particularly on his forehead. Furthermore, he looked strangely old and wrinkled. Later on, she learned that he was shorter and weighed quite a bit less than normal. An examination soon after birth showed that the baby had a heart defect, and eventually it was found that the child was mentally retarded. Maureen had given birth to a baby with Fetal Alcohol Syndrome (FAS).

If you don't know very much about FAS or perhaps have never even heard about it, don't be surprised. In fact it has only been since the early 1970s that the condition was identified and studied in the United States. The harmful effects of alcohol during pregnancy have long been suspected, however. As long ago as ancient Greece, an edict was written stating that newlyweds should not drink on the night of their marriage to avoid having defective children. At that time, it was evidently thought that drinking by the father might have an effect on the baby, but it now seems clear that it is drinking by the mother that is most likely to lead to the problem. In the sixteenth century in England it was believed that gin was the cause of weak and ill-tempered children who were sickly and shriveled and whose appearance at birth was described as old, "numbering many years."

"Starved, shriveled, imperfect" were words used by doctors and others to describe children born of alcoholic mothers in England in the mid-1800s. More recently in the United States, the phrase "a funny looking kid" has been used to describe children born of mothers who are alcoholics, alcohol abusers, or who drink heavily during pregnancy. People sometimes describe these children as having an "unfinished look" about them.

In the early twentieth century, medical researchers had the idea that there were no effects of maternal drinking upon the fetus, but in the last decade, studies have been made of infants born of mothers who consumed a lot of alcohol during the time that they were pregnant. The results of these studies have shown clearly that the drinking of alcohol, perhaps even in quite small amounts, can have damaging effects. A number of infants studied were born with a definite pattern of physical, mental, and behavioral abnormalities, which were given the name fetal alcohol syndrome.

The babies with this syndrome were shorter and lighter in weight than normal, and they failed to catch up to their brothers and sisters in growth and development even when they were given special postnatal care. They also had abnormally small heads and irregularities of the head and face. They had ear abnormalities such as crinkling of the ear, tilting of the ear backward on the head, a short bridge of the nose with upturned nostrils, and flattened or absent ridges on the upper lip. Such babies were found to have narrow vermillion borders of the upper lip, short upper and lower jaws, and faulty teeth often having a poor quality of enamel. Because of the extra folds on the upper eyelids, the eyes appear smaller than normal.

PHYSICAL CHARACTERISTICS

Small head
Ears that are crinkled
and tend to rotate backwards
Eyes that appear small because
of an excess of tissue around them
Short, upturned nose
Shortened upper jaw
Flattened ridges under the nose
Narrow upper lip
Teeth that are small and with
faulty enamel
Short length from top of head
to rump
Low weight
Inmature fingernails
Limited elbow movement
Smaller than normal little finger
Occasional hernias of diaphragm,
umbilicus or groin
Heart defects

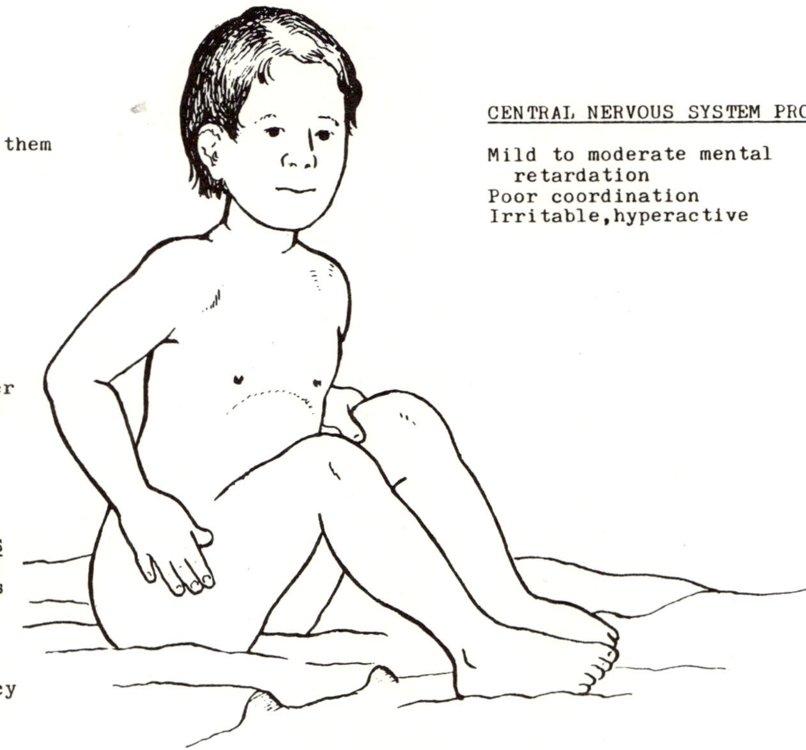

CENTRAL NERVOUS SYSTEM PROBLEMS

Mild to moderate mental
retardation
Poor coordination
Irritable,hyperactive

OTHER OCCASIONAL CHARACTERISTICS

Missing, extra or webbed fingers
Bony abnormalities or fusions
Altered palmar creases
Genital abnormalities
Hollow chest
Unusual amount of hair in infancy
(Hirsutism)
Cleft lip or cleft palate

Figure 10. Features of fetal alcohol syndrome.

According to Dr. Paul C. Orr, Assistant Professor in the Department of Psychiatry, Medical College of Pennsylvania, other abnormalities that may occur in the syndrome are heart defects and bone irregularities or fusions of the neck vertebrae. The child with the syndrome may have misssing, extra, or webbed fingers, a shorter than usual little finger, unusual-looking creases of the palm of the hand, and abnormalities of the genitals. Still other problems may be limited movement of the elbow, poorly formed fingernails, and hernias of the diaphragm, umbilicus, or groin.

The babies may be irritable at birth, nurse poorly sometimes showing an inability to grasp and suck on the mother's nipples, and are often sickly, nervous, and overactive. Dr. Orr, who is studying the syndrome, says that the greatest tragedy for the children and their parents, however, is the mental retardation the children suffer. Their IQs range between 40 and 80 with the average being about 68. Some infants are born with practically all of the characteristics we have described, although, fortunately, most show only some of the abnormalities.

It may be difficult to believe that alcohol can bring about such harmful effects on the unborn baby, and an understanding of how alcohol interacts with the fetus may be beneficial. Marian Sandmaier, writting in the Public Health Service leaflet *Alcohol and Your Unborn Baby*, points out that when a pregnant woman takes a drink, the alcohol readily crosses the placenta to the fetus. Since the alcohol travels through the baby's bloodstream in at least the same concentration as that of the mother, the mother who gets drunk causes her baby to become intoxicated as well.

The developing liver of the unborn baby can process alcohol at less than half the rate of the adult liver. This means that the alcohol remains in the fetal system much longer than in the adult system. As Sandmaier stresses, unfortunately for the fetus, it can't speak up and say no when it has had enough. Furthermore, for the fetus, even a very small amount of alcohol may be to much.

It appears that the mental retardation suffered by some babies born to women who drink excessively may stem from periods of oxygen deprivation to the uterus. Researchers at the National Institute of Child Health and Human Development report that studies with monkeys reveal that alcohol can severely restrict blood flow through the umbilical cord, which carries nutrients to and from the fetus. According to the researchers, this transitory collapse of umbilical cord vessels results in periods of acute oxygen deprivation to the fetus and also increases the acid levels of its fluids.

With this information in mind, the expectant mother who may be accustomed to having a drink or two when she goes out to dinner, watches TV, or goes to a cocktail party will have a number of questions about how to handle drinking during pregnancy. She should realize that it just can't be predicted to what extent the fetus she is carrying will be affected by her drinking. She should also be aware that if she has a martini, so does her child.

There is still a great deal that is not known about this matter, including the risks of small amounts of alcohol, moderate drinking, and periodic heavy drinking. Other questions are whether the fetus is most susceptible to alcohol at a particular time during pregnancy and whether FAS is associated with other risk factors such as the nicotine in tobacco and poor nutrition.

Although alcoholism with heavy drinking during pregnancy has been a consistent factor in cases of FAS, other risk factors may make a woman more likely to deliver an FAS child. Smoking, other drug use, and alcoholism of the father are other risk factors, all of which are less well understood than is the mother's alcoholism.

It now appears that women who drink even quite small amounts of alcohol during pregnancy may risk harmful effects on their unborn children. In recent testimony before a Senate subcommittee, Dr. Edward Brandt, Assistant Secretary of Health, Department of Health and Human Services, said that alcohol consumption at the level of two drinks per day is asssociated with decreased birth weight and behavioral defects. Increased spontaneous abortions have also been noted for women who report drinking one or two drinks per day.

The surgeon general of the U.S. Public Health Service has stated that the safest policy is to avoid alcohol entirely during pregnancy. In an advisory announcement to workers in the health field issued in July 1981, the surgeon general informed the staff members that pregnant patients should be told about the risk of alcohol consumption during pregnancy and advised not to drink alcohol. The pregnant woman should also find out about the alcohol content of food and drugs she may be taking, the advisory message warned. It concluded with the information that alcohol consumption during pregnancy, especially in the early months, can harm the fetus.

A study conducted for the National Council on Alcohol Abuse and Alcoholism brought out that women regard their doctors as the most credible sources of information about pregnancy, even more credible than other women who have had babies. According to women questioned in the survey, some doctors say that it is all right to drink during pregnancy, which indicates that a few physicians at least may not be as familiar with FAS as they should be. The study also indicated that women are fearful about complications of pregnancy and are particularly concerned about giving birth to a handicapped child.

Still another finding was that pregnant women and their husbands have the idea the symptoms of FAS are reversible and that the FAS characteristics will disappear after the baby has been born and is no longer influenced by the mother's drinking as it was during the fetal state. They think that the baby will soon "dry out." The truth is, of course, that the symptoms are not reversible and will remain for life with the person who suffers from the syndrome.

In conclusion, because there are many unanswered questions about FAS, the safest policy is not to drink at all during pregnancy. For those who continue to drink and for others concerned with the problem, the questions still to be answered include Is one heavy bout of drinking enought to cause the syndrome? Does a woman who has a history of heavy drinking face a greater chance of bearing a child with FAS? Is there a critical period during pregnancy when heavy drinking is more likely to produce the syndrome, and if so, is it during periods of organ formation, cell growth, or general growth in weight? Do persons with FAS have a normal life expectancy? What happens to them as they mature into adolescence and later into adulthood? Because FAS was described in the United States only as recently as the early 1970s, there have been no long-term studies that can answer these perplexing questions.

Adding to the quandary is that most birth defects are caused during the first 12 weeks of pregnancy when a baby's arms, legs, internal organs, and brain are being formed. The wrong drug taken at this time could damage the baby's development. There is the possibility that Fetal Alcohol Syndrome is most likely to take place if drinking is done early in pregnancy. Of course, women usually do not know they are pregnant until weeks or even months after conception takes place, and they may well continue to persist in their drinking habits during that time.

There have been a number of studies about the frequency of the syndrome. Studies in Boston have indicated the frequency to be one in 1,800 births. Dr. Paul C. Orr believes the frequency to be as high as one in 1,000. Studies by the National Council on Alcoholism, however, show that the syndrome may occur as often as one in every 750 births. Furthermore, NCA states that FAS is the third leading cause of congenital conditions in infants in the nation, followed by Down's syndrome and spina bifida. A Swedish survey reported one FAS in 600 births in that nation, and in France one FAS in 400 was reported if all cases were counted, one in 1,000 if only severe cases were included.

At least one estimate placed the number of infants born in the U.S. alone with the full fetal alcohol syndrome in a single year at 6,000 with another 24,000 infants suffering fetal alcohol effects.

It is evident that much more needs to be learned about FAS. Answers to many of the questions about the syndrome will have to await the results of studies such as those being conducted at the Medical College of Pennsylvania and at other research centers throughout the world.

In the meantime, by making informed, thoughtful decisions about the matter based on what is presently known, the woman of child bearing age can greatly increase her chances of having a healthy, normal baby!

Figure 11. Fetal alcohol syndrome (FAS) may occur as often as one in every 750 live births.

Chapter 6

DRUGS AND SEXUALITY

IN the January 1982 edition of *Listen* magazine, the question is raised, "What do drugs and sex and oil and water have in common?" The answer, according to the magazine: "These duos just don't mix well."

You may have heard stories about how the use of drugs makes sex even better. The truth is that in many cases, especially among people who use drugs frequently, interest in sex may grow less and may even die completely. In the book *Sex Education for Physically Handicapped Youth*, the authors point out that people who use drugs often grow so interested in their habit that it becomes their most important concern. The main interest of heroin users, for example, is in getting a daily supply of heroin, and their interest in such things as sex fades. Women who are using heroin heavily often consider sex a secondary activity, one that has low priority.

Many men who are being treated for heroin addiction by being given methadone may complain of problems with their sexual performance. The fact that research has not supported biochemical or physical effects on sexual ability does not diminish the real problem these individuals have. It points up the complexity of helping people attain a satisfactory sex life.

Drugs are sometimes taken by people who have problems with their sexual performance and think that drugs will help them overcome their troubles. Others, even though their sex life is quite normal, believe it can be made even better by resorting to drugs. It is, of course, dangerous for anyone to take an unknown medication without a prescription in an effort to improve sexual performance. The best advice for people who are having sexual problems is to consult a physician or a counselor.

The purpose of this chapter is to give a few details about the effects of drugs on sexuality and to point out that almost all of these effects impair not only sexual relations but also other contacts between males and females. This chapter is titled "Drugs and Sexuality" for a specific purpose. Sexuality is much more than just sexual intercourse, since the greater part, by far, is the rest of the spectrum of sexuality, which deals with playing the role of a boy or a girl, man or woman, husband or wife and enjoying sexual compatibility.

These constitute the main sexual roles, which go far beyond the sex act. They form a way of life that includes a lot more than experiences in the bedroom. Sexuality involves a secure sense of self and willingness to be self-expressive. In *The Sex Game,* Jessie Bernard considers even a broader view of man and woman relationships in which sexuality is just one part of the whole system of conversations, signs and actions taking place between human beings to declare one's interest and to follow up with appropriate action. This entire complicated system can be badly affected by the use of alcohol or other drugs.

A great variety of drugs can have a harmful effect upon sexuality. Hallucinogenic drugs such as PCP can make sex a bad or frightening experience rather than a pleasant one because the drugs can make people violent. This is particularly true if the male sex partner is taking the drug. The hallucinogens can cause sexual dysfunction and impotence and can lead to permanent brain impairment. Personal safety is always at risk when people who are intoxicated engage in sex.

In their nationally syndicated column, Drs. James Comer and Alvin Poussaint point out that there are many myths being circulated about the so-called aphrodisiacs, which supposedly improve sexual performance. A number of popular sexually oriented magazines carry advertisements for these products. These advertisements promise miraculous results in sexual performance and recommend the use of substances for all kinds of sexual fantasies and ailments. Most of these products are completely worthless and

Figure 12. Human sexuality involves a great variety of activities such as getting acquainted, going to school together, and dating.

some are actually harmful. The main interest of their manufacturers is in making profits from naive and gullible people whose sex lives are inadequate.

Perhaps you've heard that certain kinds of drugs make an individual more sexually potent. The pills referred to may be any number of tranquilizers and sedative drugs that have the effect of making the tense and anxious person more relaxed and less inhibited. Not only do most of these drugs fail to increase potency, but they can also be addictive and, when taken in heavy doses, even life threatening.

Drs. Comer and Poussaint add that a group of drugs called volatile nitrites (poppers) may intensify the pleasure of sex, however, they do not increase sexual potency and can be dangerous. Stimulants, including amphetamines and cocaine, have been touted as enhancers of sex drive. These drugs act upon the central nervous system to speed up bodily functions. Some people find exciting the sense of blood "rushing" and increase of bodily activities that may result from the use of stimulant drugs, but the truth is that these drugs can be much more harmful than beneficial. Furthermore, their use is illegal.

Opiates such as morphine, heroin, and codeine may generally produce a feeling of happiness. They might lessen an individual's inhibitions, but they can also decrease sex drive and lead to a loss of ability to have normal sex at all. If these opiates are not prescribed by a physician, they are illegal. They are also strongly addicting.

The harmful effect of drugs on sex is a main reason why drug addicts in such countries as Pakistan seek help to break the drug habit. The importance of sexual relations in the rugged frontier towns of that country is emerging as a possible motivating factor in controlling the drug problem. Addicts have admitted to drug rehabilitation workers that their failure to perform sexually while taking such drugs as heroin has convinced them to try to break the habit. Manhood must be proved, and anything that interferes with a man's prowess cannot be tolerated for long.

One youthful Pakistani resident who was being treated in a drug abuse center in Peshawar said the real reason he had checked into the center was that he had sexual problems. He said that he couldn't function right with the heroin in him, that this brought him shame, and that he stopped being a man. He was anxious to try to kick the habit even though he admitted that when he didn't have heroin he had pain all over – in his heart, his lungs, and his liver.

A drug that is widely promoted as an enhancer of sex is marijuana. Pot has a tendency to decrease one's inhibitions and may also raise the level of suggestibility. Some people maintain that it does not interfere with performance as alcohol often does. Certain marijuana users may claim an increase in sensory perceptions and bodily awareness, which they believe improves sexual activity and aids them in better appreciating it. Many other marijuana users, however, report a disinterest in sex when "stoned." They prefer to experience their own thought and unique perceptions.

As one marijuana user explained it, "When I'm using pot, it's for reasons other than for sex. In fact, sex is usually the farthest thing from my mind when I'm smoking marijuana." His wife, who also uses pot, scoffed at the idea that marijuana improves sexual pleasure or, in fact, has anything to do with fostering interest in sex.

The book *Marihuana Today* lists a number of possibly harmful effects from the use of pot. These include a reduction in the sperm count, harmful effects on normal processes of sexual development in teenage boys, and sterility in adult male users. In addition, the book cites a study involving researchers from New England Deaconess Hospital and Harvard University Medical School showing an apparent relationship between marijuana use and gynecomastia, a feminizing change in men that includes enlargement of the breasts. Some of the men afflicted requested surgery for removal of the breast tissue. Others found that when they stopped using marijuana, there was a decrease in the size of the breasts, and they were no longer as sensitive to the touch as they had been. In addition to other problems, chronic usage of marijuana may reduce general drive and potency.

Several studies have shown a connection between tobacco use and male impotence, lowered counts of testosterone, and sterility. Tobacco use impairs sexual performance in several ways. Carbon monoxide intake cuts down the blood supply level and hinders the production of hormones. Nicotine constricts the blood vessels, the swelling of which makes up the main mechanism of sexual excitement and erection. Stamina also is reduced by heavy smoking, and the smoker may not be able to "last" during intercourse, minimizing the pleasure for both partners. Still another factor is the staining of teeth and the tainting of breath, both of which reduce the smoker's sexual attractiveness.

According to *Today's Health,* Dr. Alton Ochsner, who practiced medicine for more than a generation, had this to say about smoking and sex: "I've had literally dozens of patients tell me, almost as an afterthought that after they quit smoking, their sex lives improved."

Using data collected over a 50-year period, one researcher noted that nonsmokers seem to have more satisfactory sex lives, fewer cases of impotence, and fewer instances of lowered sperm count than do smokers. A short-term increase in impotence and a decline in sexual activity in males aged 40 and younger have been revealed in other studies. One explanation is that nonsmokers in general are in better physical health and have greater physical and psychological energy and stamina.

Of course, smoking also can have harmful effects on the wider field of sexuality. Growing numbers of people are objecting to the polluting effects of smoking on the environment, the bad effects on the nonsmoker, and the odors that saturate hair, clothing, draperies, and even furniture. As one writer expressed it in *Listen* magazine, How about the not-so-publicized effects of smoking that can barely be tested or tallied, like the human factors of like and dislike? He goes on to point out that some youths avoid dating smokers, because smokers evidently disregard their own health and the health of others.

The drug most commonly associated with sexual activity is alcohol. This drug reduces inhibitions in some people, which may make them more amorous, freer, and more relaxed in lovemaking. By taking a few drinks, some persons who are not alcoholics or heavy drinkers may experience a dulling of their sense of restraint. They may also feel less guilty about sex. At the same time, alcohol often decreases actual performance and potency. Men, in particular, have often complained of potency problems while intoxicated or nearing intoxication. The sex life of alcoholics has been revealed to be disturbed, deficient, and ineffectual. The impotence that sometimes shows up may be reversed with return to sobriety. Studies have shown repeatedly that large doses of alcohol frustrate sexual activities. The problem has perhaps never been summarized more expertly than by Shakespeare, who states that drink "provokes the desire, but it takes away the performance."

When a person has been drinking heavily and has sex, much of the enjoyment is lost, sensations are blunted, and sex just isn't as pleasant. A study at the University of Pittsburgh showed that men who drink heavily become less manly in several ways, among them being the ability to have satisfactory sex. A girl who has been drinking a great deal of wine, beer, or liquor may wake up lying next to a man she does not know and realize that she had sex but wasn't aware of it at the time. It's evident that the use of alcohol will do little to promote sexual enjoyment and in most cases will have a harmful effect upon it.

The truth of the matter is that sex is often the "cause" and drinking the effect, since alcoholism frequently stems from the inability to sustain an effective sexual relationship. According to Dr. Ruth Fox, formerly of the National Council on Alcoholism, philandering and impotence among alcoholics is much higher than in the general population, and their divorce rate is four times higher.

As far as the heavy drinker or alcoholic is concerned, he is wrapped up in himself in an unhealthy way. He has problems in communicating with others, including relating to others sexually. A man who has been drinking falls far short of being the ideal sex partner. He loses muscular control, becomes sleepy and sloppy, and may even black out. If he is able to perform sexual intercourse at all, it is often done on the instinctive level and the woman is not made to feel like an individualized partner, with an equal opportunity to enjoy the relationship.

The heavy drinking male may be uncouth, rough, and concerned with satisfying his own desires more than anything else. He may say or do things that will turn off his sex partner. Instead of have a satisfying relationship, intercourse, if achieved at all, can well be a disappointment. He may try to hurry the act, causing it to be unsatisfactory for both partners.

The book *Alcohol and Alcoholism* makes the point that while the female heavy drinker does not have to worry about becoming sexually impotent, she does risk losing her attractiveness and desirability. Excessive drinking will hinder her from taking proper care of her body and clothes. Uncombed and unwashed hair, dulled eyes, sagging hemlines, twisted stockings, messy lipstick, and spotted clothing do nothing to enhance desirability. Physical changes resulting from heavy drinking of alcohol and lack of proper food can result in bloating and weight gain, scrawny appearance and weight loss, coarsened skin, alcoholic breath, and reddened eyes. Finally, like her male counterpart, the woman who drinks heavily or who becomes an alcoholic loses interest in sex.

If she does take part in sex, she may be lethargic and unresponsive and may fall asleep or pass out. As we stressed earlier, she may have intercourse and not be aware of it, since she was not alert at the time, was not really involved in the act, and obtained no satisfaction from it. Her boyfriend or husband may not long put up with her shortcomings, which may well include shrewish behavior, temper tantrums, and illnesses resulting from heavy drinking.

Sexual intercourse is a very personal, intimate, private activity that for full satisfaction requires the cooperation of both partners. Expectation, foreplay, the act itself, and a period of afterplay when the partners relax while still in close embrace are all important. Failure to get involved in any of these steps can lead to a frustrating, disappointing experience for one or both of the partners.

If either of the partners has been drinking or using other drugs, the performance is usually much poorer than it could be. If, for example, the male partner has been using drugs, he may have premature ejaculation, impotence, or other problems. Even if the act is carried out, the female partner may not be aroused sufficiently and may not take part fully in it.

A woman who is addicted to heroin may feel that sex is not needed and not worth the energy required to reach an orgasm. Women who are heavy heroin users may regard sex mainly in terms of earning money as a prostitute to maintain their addiction. Their interest in having sex with boyfriend or husband is almost totally replaced by involvement with their addiction. Women who have a male administer heroin to them ("hit" them with heroin) say that the act takes the place of sex.

For the couple who are addicted, a common bond is found in heroin. Although there may be a kind of love relationship, it may be a brother-sister type of relationship more than anything else. According to an article in the *International Journal of the Addictions,* the addicted couple are together practically 24 hours a day and doing almost everything together: hustling, scoring, fixing, eating, and sleeping. One important element of a love relationship is almost entirely omitted, however, and that is the act of sexual intercourse. Often during the time of her addiction, the woman addict does not have an orgasm. If she has an interest in sex, she may, when she thinks it over, decide that it is just not worth the effort.

In the long run, heavy use of drugs or drug addiction can only be detrimental to sexuality as it is to other aspects of life such as earning a living or keeping in good physical condition. The heavy user of drugs retreated further and further into himself or herself, eventually shunning almost all contact with others except as it relates to obtaining and using drugs. Even the occasional user may find interest is being lost in keeping contact with friends and that interest in sex declines along with interest in many other activities that were formerly enjoyed.

For the greatest satisfaction in the larger context of sexuality as well as in the act of sexual intercourse, it is wise to stay off all kinds of drugs, including alcohol and tobacco.

Chapter 7

PREVENTION – FOR PARENTS, TEACHERS, YOUTHS, AND OTHERS

"I AM a divorcee and the mother of three kids. I have had lots of difficulties and right now I am afraid that my teenage daughter is on the way to becoming an alcoholic. Please rush me information that will help me with this problem because I am at my wit's end."

"My oldest boy is really into drugs and I'm worried that he may overdose. Mail me information about treatment centers so that I can get help for him."

"I'm a teacher at Lincoln High School. I believe that several of my students are taking drugs and I want to start a curriculum that will help them overcome this habit."

"My son-in-law goes wild when he gets drunk. Sometimes he beats up both my daughter and me. The police say that they can't do anything unless they catch him in the act and we don't want to swear out a warrant for his arrest. Can you help us?"

"I am a 14-year-old student at Washburn high school. Several of my friends are on drugs. I need to know about drugs and alcohol and what they do to you."

Letters like these are received almost on a daily basis by drug and alcohol treatment centers in all parts of the nation. Such communications indicate several things – the drug problem is widespread, parents and teachers want desperately to help, and young people are concerned not only about drug abuse among their friends but also about how drugs might affect them. Perhaps more than anything else, such pleas for help show the great need for prevention efforts. Prevention is a familiar term, particularly in the public health field. All of us at one time or another, usually starting at an early age, have participated in prevention programs such as receiving an immunization to prevent a childhood disease; drinking fluoridated water or having a topical application of flouride to avoid tooth decay; taking part in a screening program such as blood testing or a reading for high blood pressure detection; or going to a doctor for a checkup even though we have no symptoms of illness at the time. In other fields, there are also well-known prevention efforts such as defensive driving and fire safety. Prevention is a popular idea because it does work and it saves money. Speaking at a meeting of drug and alcohol officials, Dr. H. Arnold Muller, State Secretary of Health of Pennsylvania, said that prevention programs can lessen the need for treatment and should have wider support from agencies that serve substance abusers.

The prevention efforts we have described are quite clear-cut, but what really is involved in drug abuse prevention? The leaflet *Drug Abuse Prevention for You and Your Family* states that prevention is a simple concept, but it requires constant work to be successful. Drug abuse prevention requires a basic understanding and a strong commitment from parents. Prevention is a positive process. If children grow up with love and security, feel that they can express themselves freely, are realistic and yet optimistic about their abilities, and are able to make sound decisions, they may never become dependent upon drugs. Here are some of the things that you as a parent can do to help your child from becoming involved with drugs.

As a parent, you have a major responsibility to give love and affection as the child grows, starting with the earliest days of infancy. When discipline is necessary, be fair and firm, clear and consistent. Don't be harsh one day and lenient the next, since when this course is followed, the child does not know what to expect and may think they he can talk his way out of punishment. Do everything possible to keep open channels for feelings and thoughts. If a youngster comes to you with a question about sex or crime or drugs, avoid telling him that he is too young to be given information about the subject. Answer the questions with details that you think the child can understand. A child who is rebuffed may not come back to ask questions the next time something bothers him.

It is important, too, to provide opportunities for successful experiences at home and in school. Let your child paint his room if he wants to even though it means paint spills, a less-than-perfect job, and extra clean-up work for you. When a school assignment comes along, provide as much support as possible. If you can give a little extra help the child may well come home with a glowing account of how well his "show and tell" presentation went off.

A stable family atmosphere is also of great importance. In Chapter 4, we have pointed out the havoc in families caused by fights, arguments, and other abusive behavior in the home. Try not to be too upset when the child breaks a family heirloom or drops a fork in the garbage disposal. If you blow up when something goes wrong, the child may attempt to hide other mistakes, and the practice of secretiveness may transfer to such things as drug abuse.

By doing your best to be a strong and thoughtful example in the home, you will encourage the youngster to come to you with problems as well as with questions about some of the matters that may be worrying him. You can't be an expert about all subjects, but learn enough about drugs so that you don't call marijuana "a narcotic" or refer to amphetamines as "downers." When you show that you lack basic information about drugs, your child may turn to his peers or others for answers.

Mike Flourney, Director, Northern Communities Mental Health and Mental Retardation, Soft Drug Program, Pittsburgh, says that prevention is really concerned with people, not drugs. He lists needs for the individual including the need for self-appreciation; the need for esteem; the need for love, affection, and belonging; and safety, social, and psychological needs. At very young ages, these needs can well be provided within the structure of the family.

According to Mr. Flourney, family influence is the most vital factor in the development of attitudes and habits in the preschool child and even through the ages of six and seven, but for eight and nine year olds, teachers and others in the school environment begin to exert influence along with the family. For children 10 and 12 years of age, the influence of peers grows in importance and is perhaps the major factor. Youths in the 13 to 18 years age bracket in the middle school and high school are most affected by a combination of influences of family, school, and their peers. In youths above the usual high school ages, family influence fades and peer pressure becomes the paramount factor.

Figure 13. Family influence is a vital factor in the development of attitudes and habits in children.

As long as children are in the home, however, parents have a role to play in prevention, sometimes as simple as helping them find satisfying alternatives to drug abuse. If you don't already know just what it is that your children like to do best, take time to find out. Whether it's some kind of sports activity, listening to music, or whatever, take the time to do what they enjoy. Too often other things that seem more important may come along, but to prevent drug abuse, there is nothing of more value than spending time with your children.

The booklet *Drug Abuse Prevention for Your Family* states that the reasons people abuse drugs are as different as people are from one another. People take drugs to change the way they feel, to feel happy, to feel better, to feel nothing, to forget, to remember, to be accepted, to be sociable, to be something different from what they are. Drugs may seem like the best way to change a mood, to stop physical or mental pain, to increase self-assurance, to appear independent, daring, or even attractive, to escape from loneliness. It appears that youths are continually enjoying the company of their friends or having seemingly endless telephone conversations with them. At least one study, however, revealed that adolescence can be an especially lonely time of life. The extent of adolescent suicide is a possible indication that this finding is true.

People often feel differently about themselves when they use drugs, but the effects usually don't last long. In the final analysis, people who misuse or abuse drugs feel worse about themselves because their problems increase, and they often get trapped in a spiral of increasing drug use.

Within the family, many things influence a young person's attitude toward drugs and the likelihood that he will abuse them. First is the exemplar role played by the parents. Children often mimic their parents' weaknesses as well as their strengths. It is well known that twice as many children smoke in families where the parents smoke as in families where parents are nonsmokers. If a parent drinks or takes pills to deal with difficult situations or escape personal problems, to feel better or "just to have a good time," the children in the family may grow up believing that these are the right ways to react to disappointments or problems. Research shows a strong relationship between the use of drugs by parents and drug abuse in children.

By taking a personal failure or disappointment in stride, the parent can show children in the family that such episodes can be dealt with in a positive way without having to resort to pills or alcohol. Many adults find that following a major disappointment or a crisis, some sort of physical activity around the house to release tension, such as painting, making an article of clothing or a piece of furniture, or doing repair work, helps them to cope with the problem. By pursuing such a course, the parent sets a good example for the children.

Of course, parents are people too, and children can understand that no one is perfect. What they need to be shown is consistent and decent behavior in people they most admire. What can lead to confusion is the "Do as I say, not as I do" philosophy, which has been proven to be almost worthless. You as the parent are the example, and it is a most important role to play. If you rely on drugs, you may be passing on problems of your own to your children. They may not be able to handle such problems by themselves, because they are not old enough or do not have the experience to do so.

Parents also have the responsibility of setting some guidelines for their children's activities. Such guidelines may often be welcomed, since a youngster may be pressured by friends to do something or go someplace that is a cause of worry for him. Parents should know where the youth goes, who he is with, what he is doing while away from home, and what time he is to return, particularly at night. This information is gathered not because parents need to spy but because they need to share in their children's activities and show they are interested in, as well as responsible for, their children's welfare. If youths fail to follow these guidelines, action should be taken such as "grounding" the youngster – keeping him at home for a specified time following the incident.

Parents should also have a pretty good idea of just where a child is going to spend the evening. Is Mary going to a dance, a movie, to watch television with George, or to a party at Tom's house? If she is going to the party, will his parents be home? Will alcohol be served or drugs experimented with? What time will she be home and who will bring her home?

Parents also have an obligation to find out as much as they can about the crowd that their child is going with. Are any of them alcohol abusers or users of drugs? Are they likely to be drinking and driving? Have they been involved in episodes with the police? By talking to other parents, teachers and recreation and youth center directors, and youths themselves, parents can usually get answers to their questions.

The influence on young people by others of the same age or slightly older – their peers – is something that must be recognized by parents. It has been referred to as "the first great and unavoidable trial of life outside the family." At certain times in a youngster's life, the desire to be liked and accepted by peers becomes more important than the influence of the parents, as Mr. Flourney's listing of influencing factors stresses. Your child's peers, his playmates, friends, and acquaintances, can make life pleasant or extremely unpleasant. A child is judged by his or her peers with a harshness and directness not common in adult society, to insure that the child "fits." Peer pressure centers on topics parents don't always relish discussing, such as drugs and sex. However, the strength a child needs to respond wisely to some of these demands arises mainly from the home and the family.

Whenever possible, hopes that a youth has should be fulfilled even though it may strain family resources. Lisa, a 14-year-old girl, had always dreamed of owning a horse. She read articles about horses and wrote stories about them. She had even fashioned a saddle and harness from leftover articles around the house, which she hoped someday to use. Although the family lived in the city and did not have space to keep a horse, the parents finally agreed to buy a horse and arranged for the animal to be quartered at a nearby stable.

For several years, Lisa experienced the joys of owning, riding, and caring for a horse. When her main interest shifted to boys and other members of the family found that they did not particularly enjoy "mucking out" the stable, the horse was sold. Later, Lisa said that ownership of the horse had helped her through some serious trials of growing up, including peer pressure to use drugs.

The importance of peer pressure seems to be most intense during adolescence. As the mind and body develop, the innocent games of childhood are replaced by the more sophisticated entertainments of the young adult. Because adolescence is a time of questioning former values, expanding one's ideas about life, and experimentation, drug use may be attempted. Not only is it difficult for parents to discourage experimentation, such action often has a blacklash.

Helen was a 16-year-old who was dating a boy who used drugs and who encouraged her to experiment with them. Her parents tried to break up the relationship and told Helen that she should never see the boy again. Helen was not sure that she was really in love with the boy, but she deeply resented her parents forbidding her to see him. She told her girl friend that she was going to run away from home, and soon after that left her home and went away with her boyfriend. For two harrowing weeks, her parents tried to locate her, but since she had not told anyone where she was headed, there were no clear leads that could be followed.

Finally, with the aid of a private detective, Helen was found working in a fast food restaurant in a neighboring state. After she returned home, Helen realized that her parents had been deeply worried about her disappearance. Later, she went away to college, and activities she became involved in there replaced her interest in drugs.

By beginning to teach children about the use of medicines at an early age, even as young as two or three, parents can help to establish healthy attitudes toward drugs. These attitudes can come in handy later on when the children are older and are faced with a decision about abuse of drugs. As a parent, it's important for you to set a good example. Whenever you take medicine yourself or give it to one of your children, make a point of why the medicine is being taken, and how necessary it is to follow carefully the instructions on the label. Stress to the children the need to know what's in a substance, where it came from, and why it's being used before any substance is consumed.

Whenever you store medicines and hazardous substances out of the reach of children, explain that you are doing it to protect them. Explain to your children about the different uses of drugs. Using drugs properly is when prescription medicine is taken strictly in accordance with the doctor's instructions, neither more nor less than directed and at the proper times. The correct use of drugs also concerns nonprescription medicines that are taken only when needed and exactly as directed on the label or as recommended by a physician. Through proper use of drugs, family members can benefit by relief of pain, discomfort, or other signs of disease and by more rapid recovery from illness or injury.

Using drugs in wrong ways often starts with drugs that are obtained illegally. Misuse of drugs can also be the use of legally available medicines in ways not in accordance with the doctor's instructions or the directions on the label. Talk to your children about the hazards of using any drug in ways that are different from the directions on the label or another's medicine.

When children reach about eight or nine years of age, it's a good idea for parents to start talking to them about drugs. This doesn't mean that you should have the children sit down in front of you and announce, "Tonight we will talk about drugs." Choose a time when the subject comes up in the natural course of events such as a television program, a newspaper article, or a drug episode in your community. Before you begin such a discussion, make sure that you know the major drug categories, the proper names and slang names of a number of drugs, and something about the effects of each. Keep in mind that almost every youngster is likely to have a friend who is experimenting with drugs, and don't think that your child is an exception. Because youths like company, the experimenter may very well try to get his peers to use drugs.

When considering drug education for your children, there are probably two extremes that should be avoided. One is the "Good Pal" approach of being particularly chummy with the children. This has led some parents to sit down and smoke pot with their children in an effort to show that they are really "with it." The parent who tries this approach may very likely lose respect with his children, since he is not acting his age, and furthermore, he is breaking the law in their presence. The other extreme is the strict and inflexible approach – "Don't use drugs or else . . ." Based on the older age and supposedly superior knowledge of the parent, this tactic can foster bitterness and rebellion among the children.

When you do talk about drugs, make sure it's a two-way discussion. Encourage the children to express their ideas, voice their problems, and say what they really think about drug abuse and drug abusers. Parents and children discussions can be highly effective in the drug education effort.

So far, we have talked about some ideas that can help to prevent drug abuse. Some of the ideas, in fact, have been proven to be effective. In some instances, however, parents will find that prevention is not the answer, since their youngster is already into drugs. A recent call to a drug agency from an angry and worried father went something like this: "I found that my son is on hard drugs and I've been trying to beat it out of him. Two times after I had punched him and pushed him around, I had to take him to the hospital to get cuts on his face stitched up, but he's still taking drugs."

Anger or panic won't help either the drug abuser or the parent. What is needed is understanding, an open channel of communication, and a plan of action. The youth hooked on drugs needs support and understanding more than ever. Solving a drug problem as soon as it shows up is called early intervention. In many ways, the skills you as a parent need to practice early intervention are similar to skills used in prevention. You should try to understand just what your child is going through. Remember, there are a multitude of reasons why people use drugs, including changing feelings or escaping problems. Drug abuse is sometimes a symptom of a personal problem. Your child may be hurt, angry, or upset or may have started to use drugs because of peer pressures.

You may suspect drug use but may not be entirely sure that it is occurring. The best procedure here is simply to ask the questions, "Are you taking drugs because of some problem?" Try to find out what the problem is by discussing the matter calmly and openly with the youngster. You may feel that you can't deal with the matter by yourself. If doctors, clergymen, social workers, or friends have provided support in previous difficulties, don't hesitate to call for such assistance again. When drug problems occur, keep in mind that you should be patient and keep open lines of communication. Chapter 12 in this book can give you ideas on where to turn for help, and your telephone directory has iistings that can often give assistance on specific types of help.

Intervention is vital not only because continued drug abuse increases the chances of permanent harm, but in addition the effects of drugs can soon overshadow the original problem that led to the abuse. If you think that your child has a drug problem, act quickly but calmly, since your effort can make a difference in the final outcome.

In preventing drug abuse, teachers have an essential role. This includes furnishing information about drugs and also providing a forum for students to exchange ideas and come to their own conclusions.

In getting ready for a general discussion on drugs in the classroom, it is a good idea for the teacher to keep in mind that some students have very likely experimented with drugs. Such drugs would probably be amphetamines or hallucinogens, but they might also be other drugs such as narcotics. Students who have had firsthand experience with drugs may not be greatly impressed with information citing severe physical and mental hazards of drug use and abuse. In most cases, the students' experience with drugs is quite limited, and consequently, they are unaware of many of the harmful effects.

When comments are made by the students and questions raised, you as the teacher should discuss what is factual and accurate and admit that there is a lack of knowledge in regard to the effects of certain drugs. Scientific data about marijuana, for example, are still far from complete. You can serve the best interests of the students, however, if you stress that in cases where data are not complete, enough unanswered questions remain about probably damaging effects to warrant an individual staying off a drug.

To put yourself in the strongest possible position to lead a discussion, you should be well versed in the history of drugs and drug abuse. You should also be aware of the different categories of drugs, causes of drug abuse, and characteristics of drug abusers. You will be in a good position to back up your statements about drugs if you also are knowledgeable about methods of distribution of legal and illegal drugs and problems of enforcement, prevention, treatment, and rehabilitation. To counter comments made by students about use of drugs, it is also valuable to have information about drugs and the law, both at the state level and nationally.

When drug abuse is discussed, your students should be given

the chance to ask questions, give their opinions, tell about their experiences, and argue points made by others. Interest is always awakened and kept at a high level when someone who has used drugs is on hand to describe personal experiences. In Chapter 4, a visit to a health class of a student who used drugs is described.

From the standpoint of encouraging students to participate, seminars, panel discussions, and debates are always preferable and usually more valuable than formal lectures. Whatever the situation, your goal as the instructor should be to stimulate critical thinking and analysis about the subject. In such a situation, you can function most effectively as a moderator to help resolve questions that come up and see that fact is clearly established and separated from misconception and myth.

Teachers also have a role to play in intervention. They can often be the first person to detect a drug abuser because of unusual behavior in the classroom, in the corridors, or on the school grounds. As a teacher, you are always concerned with the health of your students and are alert to any changes from what is normal behavior. Particularly in your classroom from your vantage point in the front or as a monitor in moving about among the seated students, you can note such signs as unusual paleness, glassy eyes, drowsiness, general distress, illness, or unusual or erratic behavior. It is, of course, often difficult to recognize drug abusers, because signs of drug abuse, at their onset at least, are often identical to those caused by conditions having little or nothing to do with drug abuse.

Some students may, in fact, be using legitimate drugs in accordance with instructions of their physicians. Such disorders as epilepsy, diabetes, and asthma may need treatment that will bring about side effects similar to drug abuse or misuse. A student may be drowsy from taking a nonprescription drug such as an antihistamine to lessen the effects of an allergy. A clue to the possibility of drug abuse is the persistence of symptoms over days or weeks.

Although it is not always easy to recognize drug abusers, some students are potentially hard-core addicts, and they can be helped if their involvement with drugs is spotted early. It is in this way that you as a teacher can be of special aid as you concern yourself with identifying possible drug abusers. Signs that may indicate drug abuse are listed in Chapter 4.

During the school years, there are perhaps no more important individuals in the life of the student than his boy and girl friends. As a youth, what your friends do and say, how they dress, and how they react to problems all can have a profound effect upon you. In fact, actions of your friends both in school and out may have more effect upon you than any amount of statements, comments, precautions, and sermonizing voiced by parents, teachers, principals, counselors, physicians, and clergymen. Keep in mind, though, that peer influence is a two-way street. Your actions influence your friends, just as what they do affects you.

Since you are your friends' peers and they are yours, if you use or abuse drugs, you are serving as a powerful influence upon them to follow the same practices. On the other hand, if you avoid the use or abuse of drugs, you are helping to prevent drug abuse among your peers. Youths sometimes take drugs to cope with problems at home or at school. Drugs never solve problems but only serve to postpone them and usually make matters worse, because a drug problem may develop that is far more serious than the original trouble.

Once you understand what a powerful force peer influence is, you have the opportunity consciously to prevent drug problems if you only take advantage of it. You and your friends can help each other through difficult times by discussing problems that come along and by listening to one another. By avoiding drugs, you can help yourselves to a better life, one that includes natural highs from sports and other physical and social activities.

Here are some ideas on prevention from a girl in her twenties who graduated from a large city high school and then attended a community college and later a university:

> With all the programs available to help teenagers learn about drugs, you may think there's nothing you can do to help your friends make the right decision, but this is far from the truth. Teenagers are tremendously influenced by their peer group. Everyone wants to belong, and the feeling of belonging to a group is an especially strong one. You may feel that no one has ever had friends as exciting and loyal as yours, and who's to say you're wrong?
>
> This powerful bond of friendship can be used positively or

negatively. A youth should never try to hurt his friends by encouraging them to try drugs, but the fact is that this is sometimes done. Contrary to what some people may say or think, I don't believe that a friend who tries to get you to experiment with drugs is necessarily evil or deliberately trying to harm you. You can be sure, however, that when he suggests drugs use, he is acting in a thoughtless way, is using very poor judgement and does not have your best interests at heart.

It may be hard to say no to experimentation. You're at a time in your life when you're feeling very adventurous. You're just finding out about a lot of things, you have courage and energy to spare, and you want to prove yourself. There are, however, many ways of showing your fearlessness that don't involve drugs. You could say no to the PCP that's going around but yes to the road rally or ski trip or whatever way of proving yourself is popular in your neighborhood. Of course, I don't mean for anyone to go out and take unnecessary risks but to find reasonable outlets for the daring that is part of a teenager's psychological makeup.

Believe me when I say that although nobody likes a snitch, prude (or whatever terms you use when you want to put someone down), you don't have to be any of these things to oppose drug abuse. Be informed, and when you are challenged on your nonabusive behavior, you'll be able to say without being hysterical or judgemental that you won't take THC because you know that chemical analysis of what is being sold as THC has shown it to be cut with all kinds of harmful substances. You can say that you don't smoke joints because they can damage lung tissue and you prefer to have your lungs intact. You don't have to go on and on. Just give a simple and factual answer. This can be very effective and have a tremendous impact, because you as a popular person are taking a stand against drugs. Your friends will listen to you much more readily than they would a teacher or parent. Believe me, you will make an impression upon your peers, even though it may not be obvious at the time.

If a friend is deeply involved with drugs, you should help him get the assistance he needs so badly. Don't try to handle the situation all by yourself, regardless of how adequate you may feel. Your friend needs professional help that you, no matter how devoted, cannot give. Covering up your friend's problem is really not doing a good deed.

As an informed person who chooses not to take drugs, you can even help to avert a tragedy. You will realize that someone who has passed out at a party and can't be awakened may well have overdosed and needs medical help right away. Don't worry about repercussions such as parents finding out. Without medical help, your friend could suffer harm that could last a lifetime or might even die. Someone who is having a bad reaction to a drug should be given first aid and taken to the emergency room at the nearest hospital for immediate treatment. Chapter 11 gives additional details about what to do and what *not* to do.

Antidrug articles are sometimes the source of hilarity among gangs of kids and may be greeted by jokes and laughter. If your high school class is anything like mine, some clown will probably get up and yell, "All I want to know about drugs, is where to get some." It's okay to let him rave as long as you don't stop reading and learning about drugs.

The most important point of all is that using drugs or not using drugs is *your* decision. No matter how close you are to your friends, they are not you and won't suffer the consequences of *your* actions. If, supposing one of the worst scenarios, you were to drive under the influence and hit a child, injuring him so severely that he becomes brain damaged, *you*, not your friends, would have to live with the consequences. Or, more possibly, if you're caught with drugs and expelled from school, it's on your record, not your friends', and you have the hassle of getting your parents to have you reinstated. You can benefit your friends by coming out against drugs. That's what friends are for!

No one can argue with the importance of the role of youth in influencing their friends for good or bad. However, there is also a definite place for older people to help in drug abuse prevention. With years of experience in different careers and life pursuits, older adults can be a valuable resource in the fight against drugs. A vital part in the prevention of drug abuse is the help of everyone in the neighborhood in working together in renewing some of the old and proven values in raising youth – giving them companionship and attention.

What it really gets down to is taking time to do things with youngsters – sharing a favorite activity such as fishing, or practicing a craft such as carving and painting a wooden decoy duck good enough to show to friends or even to sell. Such activities furnish an opportunity for listening to youth and being a special friend to them. The art of listening has been somewhat neglected in recent years, but there's evidence of a rekindling of interest. A professor at the University of Minnesota, in fact, devoted an entire book to the art of listening, a book that apparently is being widely read.

As far as being a special friend to youth is concerned, an older adult, a person rich in years and understanding, can help a youngster become interested and involved in something other than drugs. An increase in one's own feeling of self-worth and accomplishment is a benefit gained by everyone who helps prevent drug abuse.

In the motion picture *On Golden Pond,* circumstances bring together at a lake cottage a cantankerous elderly man and a rebellious teenager. Over a period of time as the elderly man teaches the youth the lore of the outdoors, they become great friends, an experience of lasting value to both of them.

So far in this chapter, we have talked about preventive measures that can be carried out mainly by people as individuals. In quite a few communities, there are prevention efforts going on that involve groups of youths. For example, in Philadelphia, the Coordinating Office for Drug and Alcohol Abuse Programs (CODAAP) helps to furnish prevention services to youths in the schools through several outreach programs. These activities furnish alternatives to drug abuse such as discussions, role playing dramas, and neighborhood projects. More than 80,000 youths, parents, and teachers as well as community leaders benefit from these programs which are known as Project Pride, Rites of Passage, and Shalom.

To find out about such projects in your community, call or write the State Agency for Drugs and Alcohol in your state. These agencies are listed in Chapter 12.

Chapter 8

DRUGS AND DRIVING

> A 17-year-old girl was killed in an automobile accident early today on Route 23 near Brownsville when the car she was driving was struck from behind by another vehicle.
>
> A 20-year-old resident of Brownsville was charged with homicide by automobile, involuntary manslaughter, and drunken driving, according to the police.
>
> A witness to the accident said that a 1977 Plymouth being driven at a high rate of speed struck the girl's car just after she had stopped at a red light. The 20-year-old, who was not injured, was arrested at the scene. A passenger in his car, a 19-year-old girl, was hospitalized with facial lacerations and possible internal injuries.

NEWSPAPER articles similar to this story, which appeared in a metropolitan newspaper, are published by newspapers, large and small, throughout the nation. Some of the articles tell about drivers who were killed or injured by motorists who had been drinking, as this story does. Other articles describe accidents where drinking drivers careened off the road, smashed head-on into another car, swerved and overturned, or hit trees or abutments near the road and were injured or killed. Still other articles relate accidents in which pedestrians were struck and killed by drivers under the influence of alcohol. In far too many cases, the victims of these accidents are teenagers or young adults. In fact, auto accidents in which drinking is involved cause more deaths among people 35 years and under than heart disease and cancer combined.

About 52,000 fatal motor vehicle accidents occurred in 1982, and in half of them, or 26,000, drivers under the influence of alcohol were involved. Each year, the costs of motor vehicle accidents that are alcohol related amount to more than $1 billion in property damage, insurance costs, and medical services. In addition to this shocking toll of deaths, more than a half million people are injured, many of them suffering injuries that handicap them for life. Several thousand arrests are made as the result of these accidents, and thousands of drivers stand trial, lose their licenses, are sentenced to jail, or are given other sentences.

Figure 14. Drivers under the influence of alcohol were involved in 26,000 fatal motor vehicle accidents in 1982.

More than 142 million drivers are operating motor vehicles on the nations's highways and roads today, and the number is increasing at a tremendous pace as more and more poeple of all ages learn to drive. Public concern is growing over the toll of motor vehicle accidents, which are responsible for one death every 23 minutes day and night. A father who was turning over the keys to the family car to his 17-year-old son for the first time had this to say: "Remember that when you are at the wheel, you are operating a high-speed missile weighing well over a ton, capable of causing instant death and destruction not only to you and your friends, but also to others." This father had good reason for his words of caution. About 25 percent of all drivers are under the age of 25, but they have one-third of all accidents. Furthermore, boys are more likely to be involved in accidents than girls.

On modern, crowded superhighways, motor vehicles including trucks and buses are traveling at speeds approaching a mile a minute or more. The slightest deviation from the driver's course of even a few inches can result in an accident, possibly a head-on crash. Only those drivers who are completely alert and in entire control of their faculties are in condition to drive under such circumstances. Even a very small amount of alcohol can affect an individual's driving ability and cause an accident, whether the driving is being done on a city street, an expressway, or a country lane. One drink may affect a driver's judgement and may hinder his normal alertness. It may make a driver overconfident, careless, and more likely to take chances such as running a red light, passing on a curve, or speeding.

Drinking and driving accidents are the number one cause of death among teenagers. More than 8,000 youths are killed in alcohol-related motor vehicle accidents each year, and about 40,000 suffer disabling injuries. Not only are they inexperienced in driving, not having developed the techniques and knowledge that help adults out of a difficult spot in traffic, but they are also inexperienced in drinking. They do not fully realize what the effects are and how they will react to alcohol in different situations. When teenagers drink and drive they place themselves in double jeopardy.

If you ask how much you can drink and still drive safely, the answer, simply put, is nothing. Drinking alcohol seriously interferes with judgement, muscle coordination, vision, and reaction time. All of these functions are very important for driving. Alcohol has especially harmful effects upon judgement, which in turn affects decision making and risk taking. Driving requires the ability to assimilate a great amount of information in an extremely limited amount of time. A driver in city traffic may be confronted with other automobiles, buses, trucks, emergency vehicles, highway maintenance crews, and pedestrians sometimes simultaneously. Obviously, he must keep tabs on a number of moving

Figure 15. More than 8,000 youths are killed in alcohol-related motor vehicle accidents every year, and 40,000 suffer disabling injuries.

objects at the same time. The ability to track these objects can be seriously affected by alcohol.

As the Book *You . . . Alcohol and Driving* stresses, judgement guides your behavior in driving as it does in all decisions. It enables you to think clearly and to make rapid, correct decisions. In driving, judgement is in operation in every task and is at work to answer such questions as How fast am I going? How fast is the other car going? Is there time to pass? Where are the other cars in relation to my car? If the driver in front of me comes to a dead stop, can I stop without crashing into him? In a drive of a few minutes, a driver must process hundreds of pieces of information, 20 percent or more of which represent critical decisions. If these are not handled in exactly the right way, an accident can result.

The point here is that your judgement is the first important driving ability affected by alcohol. The first drink you take affects it, and it is markedly affected by about three drinks. With your judgement impaired by alcohol, you begin to take chances by driving too fast, tailgating, passing without enough time to avoid oncoming traffic and swing back into your lane safely, and making turns at too great a speed. To make things even more hazardous for you, alcohol influences your ability to judge how well you are driving. Alcohol always makes you think that you are in greater control than you actually are.

Of course, sometimes an individual is well aware that he has had too much to drink and tries to compensate for it. One youth who had been served several strong cocktails by a girl friend drove home right after having the drinks. He tried to compensate for his consumption of alcohol by stopping at every corner and creeping along between stops. Although he finally reached home safely, he was almost struck by another car as he turned into his driveway. He had been driving without his headlights.

As the publication *Alcoholism* points out, one of the main faculties of the body used in driving, vision, is especially affected by alcohol, requiring more time to adjust to brightness. A drinking driver might not be able to filter out the glare of oncoming headlights and will have to "steer blind" for several hundred feet, a matter of time and distance that could lead to a disaster. At the same time, eyes of the drinking driver are less sensitive to brilliant colors such as red. When a traffic light turns red, the drinking driver might need more time than usual for his brain to send the message to step on the brakes. Again, the extra time, if even a fraction of a second, could be enough to cause an accident.

Human vision is controlled by a very complex and delicate system that gives the eye its movement and focus. Anything that delays these responses will result in the brain getting a fuzzy picture from the eyes. Alcohol reduces the eye muscles' ability to control the amount of light entering the eye. Like camera film, too much light or not enough ruins the picture. This impairment can be caused by such factors as faulty depth perception, poor

youngsters aged 12 to 17 have a "serious drinking problem." This is defined as drinking at least once a week and consuming 5 to 12 drinks on a single occasion, just double the adult figures. The 1981 National High School Senior Survey revealed that two out of five of the 12th graders surveyed admitted they'd had five or more drinks at least once during the preceding two weeks. One out of three said that most of their friends had been drunk during the same period.

The teenager's most popular beverage, beer, is considered by most youths as being not much more potent than a soft drink. The NIAAA reports that most people – especially teenagers – just do not realize that a 12-ounce can of beer contains the same amount of alcohol as a full glass of wine or a 1-ounce shot of whiskey. To make the situation even more alarming, many teenagers freely admit to drinking and driving.

Figure 16. Teenagers often fail to realize that a 12-ounce can of beer contains the same amount of alcohol as a full glass of wine or a 1-ounce shot of whiskey.

Although the drinking driver causes far more deaths and disabling injuries and traffic safety violations than any other kind of driver, alcohol is not the only cause of "intoxication." National, state, and local officials are concerned about the growing threat of drivers under the influence of other drugs. These drugs range from the true narcotics to stimulants, tranquilizers, sleeping pills, and even some cold remedies such as antihistamines. Some drugs are widely used in such common ailments as nervousness, overweight, high blood pressure, and hay fever. Because of these everyday uses, many people are unaware of the effects these drugs have on driving ability. Due to this lack of knowledge, they may innocently contribute to the dangers on the streets and highways.

Unfortunately, there isn't a test such as the alcohol breath test for measuring drug use at the scene of an accident. The presence of drugs in the bodies of victims of fatal accidents can, of course, be determined. What is most needed is a test for determining the presence of marijuana in a driver surviving an accident, since this drug is often used and, in fact, is second only to alcohol as the drug most frequently found in the bodies of accident victims.

According to the leaflet *Drugs and Driving* published by the Food and Drug Administration, dangerous drugs are sometimes obtained, in spite of legal requirements against them, by people who use them for their side effects or other reasons than those for which they are intended. One example is the use by drivers of stimulant drugs to keep them awake.

Controlled use of drugs by a person under his doctor's care gives certain safeguards to avoid dangers of drug misuse and abuse. Uncontrolled use of the drugs we are discussing represents a danger to the health and welfare of the user and the safety of others. Because these hazards exist, there are a number of precautions that should be taken while driving.

Amphetamines have many nicknames, some of which are innocent sounding, such as "bennies," "pep pills," "thrill pills," or "copilots." Nicknames tend to make them seem harmless when, in fact, they can pose serious dangers. As we have pointed out, amphetamines are useful in treating certain illnesses when taken under the direction of a physician. Carelessly used, they can be very harmful to the health of the user and make it unsafe to drive a motor vehicle. Amphetamines give the driver a false sense of security and alertness and often increase self-confidence, which makes the taking of risks more likely.

For the protection of the user, amphetamines can be sold legally only upon a doctor's prescription by a licensed pharmacist. Anyone who avoids the requirement of a prescription by using illegal channels not only violates the law but also runs the risk of becoming "hooked" to habitual use with all the misery that can follow.

You may have heard from aquaintances that amphetamines are "no more harmful than a cup of coffee" and that by taking amphetamines "you can drive without sleep and never miss it." Both of these statements show ignorance about the facts, and both are dangerous beliefs. Amphetamines may increase alertness and efficiency for a short time and may briefly improve driving skills, but this affect can be followed by agitation, irritability, decreased attention span, and great fatigue.

The most important fact for you as a driver to think about is that excessive, unsupervised use of amphetamines interferes with the body's protective feelings of drowsiness and tiredness. When you have these feelings, your body is telling you that you need rest and you need it right away. The use of amphetamines short-circuits feelings of exhaustion, causing a driver to use up reserves of body energy until a total and sudden collapse takes place. Even before this acute stage of exhaustion is reached, there will likely be a period of decreasing driving ability and alertness accompanied by edginess. This is the time when accidents can very easily occur, even though the driver believes he is in complete control and driving efficiently.

Another reported effect is that you may see objects on the road that are not really there. These highly dangerous "mirages" or hallucinations are similar in some ways to the effects of delirium tremens suffered by the alcoholic. Such "mirages" can cause the driver to sideswipe an oncoming vehicle, have a head-on collision, or drive off the road.

Truck drivers and others such as salesmen who constantly drive back and forth across the nation's highways may try to stretch out their driving time by taking amphetamines. Reliance on these stimulant drugs can result in anything from a heart that is forced to overwork to sudden death on the highway in an accident. One study found that heavy amphetamine users were four times as likely to be involved in a car crash.

Barbiturates are useful medicines in calming nervousness and promoting sleep in people with health problems. The drugs are habit forming, and by law, may only be sold by prescription. Uncontrolled use can lead to addiction more serious in some ways than true narcotic addiction. Barbiturates are often pushed by dealers who encourage experimentation, knowing full well that it may lead to habituation and possible addiction to true narcotics.

In an effort to slow down and get off the "jag," the individual who has been using amphetamines excessively may turn to the use of barbiturates. The cycle of amphetamine-barbiturate use may become a continuing practice, causing both serious emotional and physical damage.

Heavy use of barbiturates produces symptoms similar in some ways to alcohol intoxication. The person affected becomes drowsy and confused, cannot coordinate his muscles when he walks or stands, and sometimes reaches the point of collapse. He may suffer tremors of his hands, lips, and tongue and have difficulty in thinking or talking clearly. Skills important to safe driving such as alertness, attention, judgement, and reaction times may be affected for several hours after taking barbiturates.

Even the occasional user of barbiturates will become drowsy and less alert, although the effects vary greatly from one person to another. Even if the dose is small and the time under medication limited, the person should make sure he knows how the drug will affect him before he attempts to drive. It is the doctor's responsibility, of course, to give the necessary instructions to the patient when barbiturates are prescribed.

The term tranquilizer is applied to a group of drugs that are generally prescribed to relieve tension and anxiety. Tranquilizers are central nervous system depressants that affect certain reflexes. Their effect is mainly upon a person's attitude and outlook, although some of these drugs lower blood pressure. In normal or larger doses, tranquilizers may result in sedation to the point of dizziness or drowsiness.

The most widely prescribed tranquilizers are the benzodiazepines. Therapeutic doses of diazepam may slightly alter psychomotor skills by slowing reaction time, interfering with eye-hand coordination, and affecting the speed by which the brain processes sensory information. Persons on diazepam seem somewhat less likely to check "roadway" conditions. A widely prescribed sleeping pill is flurazepam (Dalmane®). This drug accumulates in the body, and its residual affects driving skills. Elderly people should take special care when driving the day after taking this drug. Since tranquilizers pose a danger to the driver, they should be taken only under medical supervision, and the doctor should be informed that the individual is planning to drive.

Antihistamines are used for the relief of nasal congestion due to colds and to combat allergies, among other purposes. Some may be bought without prescription, while others are too dangerous for use without medical supervision. Side effects may result in attention, confusion, and drowsiness. In fact, certain antihistamines are used to help promote sleep. If the drug produces adverse results in a particular individual, he should not drive or use power machinery. If you are using antihistamines, observe the directions on the label very carefully or follow the advice of your doctor about driving or tackling other tasks that require concentration or attention.

Marijuana is a drug about which there is a great deal of controversy. Although, as we have pointed out, marijuana can have beneficial effects when used in treating certain illnesses, it can also be harmful. Studies show that subjects under the influences of marijuana are more likely to miss important visual cues when driving a motor vehicle. They also tend to have narrower fields of vision and to be a little less coordinated. Furthermore, they may experience more trouble, "tracking" or staying in their traffic lane, and they do not react as quickly to sound. It is well known that marijuana can affect judgement and concentration.

The harmful effects of marijuana may also be more lasting than those of alcohol. The National Institute on Drug Abuse (NIDA) reports that after smoking one marijuana cigarette, an individual may experience a marked decrease in driving skills over a period of five or six hours. The impairing effects of one glass of beer usually disappear after one hour. Some people believe that marijuana users try to compensate by taking fewer risks and that regular users are likely to show less impairment in driving skills than inexperienced users.

Some youths say that they feel perfectly safe driving with someone who is high because such individuals drive safely. This feeling may be based upon an illusion, however. The stoned driver may concentrate on one aspect of driving such as staying well within the speed limit, giving both the driver and passengers the idea that he's driving carefully. The total involvement of the driver with only one facet, a typical feature of the high, means that he does not pay sufficient attention to the many other elements needed for safe driving.

While marijuana by itself can spell trouble, the combination of marijuana plus alcohol can add up to a deadly situation. In a study done by the Pittsburgh Institute for Driver Research, a low dosage of alcohol was used. Subjects in the study had a BAC of .06. One joint was the highest dose of marijuana employed in the study. In one of the tests in the study, an officer experienced in traffic was asked to pull over those drivers he would have stopped for DUI (Driving Under the Influence) if they had been on the open road. Which driver had which dose of what drug was not known to the officer. He pulled over everyone who consumed both alcohol and pot, but only 25 percent of those on pot but no alcohol, and 20 percent of those on alcohol but no pot.

Because the opium derivatives, called opiates, are used primarily by doctors who treat seriously ill patients who are usually hospitalized, it is unlikely that such persons would be operating a motor vehicle. In the very few instances in which a narcotic/opiate medication is prescribed and the doctor permits the patient to drive, the physician should carefully outline the precautions. A narcotic addict or a person experimenting with these powerful drugs is, of course, a terrible threat to highway safety if he or she gets behind the wheel of an automobile.

Most individuals are well aware of the hazards of driving while under the influence of alcohol, and many people know about the dangers of the drugs we have just described. Fewer people, however, understand the perils caused by the combined effects of drugs and alcohol considered on other pages of this book. Even fewer know that cigarette smoking can have a bad effect upon how the body uses certain drugs, still another reason why smokers should give up the habit.

The combined effect of drugs and alcohol, which is known as a synergistic reaction, may be dangerous to your safety on the highway to a greater degree than the effects of either the drugs or the alcohol.

Here are a few suggestions that may save your life or the life of the driver in the next automobile –

If you are ill, see your doctor.

If your doctor prescribes drugs, ask him about driving while on the medication.

If you drink, don't drive. Ask your doctor about the combined effect of alcohol and any medication he prescribes.

Don't ask your pharmacist to violate the law by selling dangerous drugs without a prescription, and don't buy from one who will.

NEVER purchase drugs at service stations or bus stops.

If you are using nonprescription drugs, read the label carefully and follow to the letter the precautions listed.

What action can you as an individual take to deal with the problem of drugs and driving? All of us are concerned about the problem, but what can we do as individuals? At first, you may react by thinking that the problem is just too big. As you think about it, however, you may well come to the realization that there is a lot that you can do. First of all, don't drive and use drugs yourself. In this way, you are not only protecting yourself, your relatives, and friends, but you are also setting a good example for them.

As a host or hostess, you can take certain steps to insure that your guests are not involved in an accident due to alcohol consumption. If you serve alcoholic beverages in your home, it's always a good idea to furnish plenty of food. Not only do snacks make a tasty addition to your party, but they can also slow down the rate at which the body burns alcohol. This is particularly true of high protein foods such as cheese, nuts, and eggs.

When mixing drinks, always use a jigger to measure the alcohol. If your guests mix their own drinks, be sure that there are several jiggers handy. It's easy to underestimate the amount of alcohol you pour into a glass filled with ice, and that is especially true after you've had a few drinks. So at your own party, take care that your own drinking of alcohol is limited, if it is done at all.

Have a choice of nonalcoholic beverages available for guests who want them. Some people accept an alcoholic drink for the sake of being polite but actually would rather have a soft drink, fruit juice, or just plain coffee or tea.

Never force drinks on your guests, and don't permit others to coax nondrinkers to drink. This can be embarrassing for everyone on the scene and should always be discouraged. Don't be in any rush to fill glasses as soon as they are emptied. Usually the average person can only absorb about one drink an hour. Keep your eye on your guests so that you can protect them if necessary. If one of your guests is drinking too much, start a conversation with the individual, offer some food, ask him if he would like to join in a game some of the others are playing. Remember, drinks should be poured lighter as the evening progresses. Using 80 proof alcohol instead of 100 proof lowers the load taken by your guests.

Finally, shut down the bar about an hour before the party ends to give your guests time to absorb the alcohol they've consumed before they start the drive home. If you find that one of your guests has been drinking too heavily despite your precautions, it's up to you to take charge. Take some kind of action, even though it may make the individual angry. Remove the car keys from pocket or handbag and hide them. Disconnect a battery cable. If all else fails, arrange to have your guest driven home or have the person stay overnight at your home. Your guest will likely thank you later for your efforts, even though he may be annoyed at the time.

You should keep in mind, however, that taking care of an intoxicated person can be a real responsibility. Somewhere between .15 percent and .30 percent BAC, the intoxicated individual may lose consciousness and "pass out." Such a person is in a coma, and everything except the automatic processes such as breathing and heartbeat is paralyzed. This, of course, is an extremely serious matter. The individual will stay in a coma until the body burns enough alcohol so that the nerve centers controlling consciousness can operate again. It's not easy to determine whether a person has passed out or is simply sleeping it off. Try to arouse the person. If he responds by speaking or by trying to resist, he is probably just asleep. Check him again before long, however, just to be sure he hasn't gone into a coma from the alcohol already in his stomach.

If you can't arouse the person, he is probably in a coma. A person in a coma is flirting with death. He might vomit and choke to death, or he may have unabsorbed alcohol in his stomach. The BAC will increase as absorption continues. If the BAC reaches the .50 percent level or close to it, breathing may stop. Get medical help at once or take the individual to the nearest emergency room. Chapter 11 gives information on first aid measures.

Medical help is also needed for the intoxicated person who shows other signs and symptoms such as turning pale, becoming very red in appearance, or breathing irregularly. If you have to move the victim, make sure you have other people on hand to aid in restraining the person if he becomes active or violent.

A method to help prevent accidents is to place a bowl by the front door and ask guests when they arrive to drop their car keys into the bowl. Before they leave, try to determine whether they are in condition to drive. Keep on hand a supply of "Drive Alive Balloons." These are blown up by the guest and tested by a special device that registers BAC readings. Any guest whose BAC registers more than .05 should not have his keys returned until he is clearly in condition to drive. Information about where to purchase the balloons can be obtained from your local branch of the National Safety Council or the National Council on Alcoholism.

Serving alcohol to youthful guests can lead to serious problems. Not only is it illegal to serve alcohol to minors, in some states you may be sued if an accident is caused by a youngster who drank alcohol in your home!

There are many other things you can do to protect yourself, your friends, and others from drugs and driving situations. If you and your friends are going to a party, arrange in advance for one person in the group to be the driver on the return trip. This alerts the driver-to-be to the need of avoiding drinking to carry out his responsibility. One cardinal rule to follow is always to avoid driving with someone who has been drinking and encourage your friends to observe the same rule.

As a parent, what can you do to help prevent your child from being involved in drinking and driving situations? Some parents dismiss the whole idea with a wave of the hand and the comment that "Greg (or Marla) never drinks." Before you put aside the thought that your son or daughter could be involved in a drinking and driving accident, think about the results of a recent nationwide survey of 15-to-19-year-old high school students. A surprising 50 percent said that they had been in one or more situations in the past months when alcohol was present. Forty percent of the youths were girls. Remember, too, that victims of driving under the influence accidents include passengers as well as drivers. Even if your youngster never drinks, there is no certainty that he or she will not be involved in a drinking and driving episode.

Consider your own attitudes and actions and decide how they may reflect on your ideas about what your child does. How do you deal with drinking in the home, for example? What does your teenager think about your use of alcohol, and do you always show good judgement about drinking and driving yourself? How you act will probably have a lot to do with how your child thinks and behaves. If you must take certain steps because a guest at one of your parties drinks too much, explain to your child why you followed a certain course in handling the matter.

You may want to consider under what, if any, circumstances you would approve of your teenager drinking. Only under your watchful eye at a family celebration such as a wedding? At neighborhood affairs closely supervised by adults, preferably close friends of yours? At the home of teenage friends only if the parents are present? Or not at all? Your feelings about drinking should be clearly explained to your youngster.

Although you will have many concerns about your child being

involved in drinking and driving, your first concern naturally is your child's safety. When you are sitting at home at 3 AM waiting for your son or daughter to return from a date and you hear the sound of an ambulance siren, you hope and perhaps pray that it's not your youngster who is injured. Besides your concern about an accident, you are also likely to be worried about your child getting sick, fighting, or damaging his or her reputation. Other worries may include the possibility of pregnancy or other sex-related problems or of being arrested.

Many attempts to reduce teenage drinking and driving haven't been very successful. Horror stories of accidents seem to turn adolescents off in many cases. Most seem to feel, "It won't happen to me or my friends." Attempts to restrict the use of the car or of choice of friends also appear to have limited value. Teenagers are pretty much on their own once the car leaves the driveway and they head for the party, the drive-in, or the game.

Nevertheless, keep in mind that driving and the use of drugs is a subject that your teenager probably wants you to talk about. A recent nationwide survey carried out for the National Highway Traffic Safety Administration found that teenagers expect and want their parents to discuss with them drinking and driving. Most teenagers are worried about the problem and want advice from you, although they may never come right out and ask for it. A basic element in a successful drunk driving survival program for your family is communications, based upon a sympathetic realization of the problems with which youth must contend.

You were young yourself once, perhaps not too long ago, and it helps to refresh your memory about how you felt and acted when you were up against some of the same kinds of problems that your child faces now. Of course, drugs were probably not as much of a problem when you were a teenager as they are now, but there were other difficulties for which parallels can be drawn.

Use everyday happenings such as news events to get the conversation underway. Once you have broken the ice, it should be easier to pick up on the conversation whenever it seems appropriate.

Talk to your children without lecturing them or making them feel that they are on the witness stand. Some youths complain that when their parents talk to them about drugs, sex, or similar topics the adults do all the talking and the youths can barely get a word in edgewise. Honest two-sided communication between you and your teenagers is a key to dealing with this matter. Give your children a chance to express their ideas. It's never a good idea, of course, to start a conversation on drugs and driving when your son or daughter comes home under the influence. A discussion the next morning has a much better chance for success.

The Public Health Service Leaflet *Talking to Your Teenagers About Drinking and Driving* points out that the subject can best be considered when family members are in a calm frame of mind. Make it clear that you want to share some ideas about drinking and driving and that you are not about to make any accusations or hand out ultimatums. Read as much as you can about the subject so that you can include some hard facts in your comments.

Find out exactly what your children think about the problem. Ask them what they would do if a friend had too much to drink and insisted upon driving regardless of his condition. Would they be willing to call home despite the lateness of the hour to ask someone to pick them up? In some communities organizations have been formed that arrange for parents to pick up youths in such situations, with no questions asked at the time. You might suggest the possibility of the "buddy system" used in swimming, where one person assumes responsibility for protecting the life of the other. A recent study revealed that youths are deeply concerned about drinking among their friends and that the great majority of teenagers are more than willing to take over the driving to protect their friends.

Talk about the laws governing drinking in your community, laws that are likely to get stricter as part of the nationwide effort to deal more sternly with drivers under the influence. What are the consequences of breaking laws – arrest by the police, trial or hearing, loss of license for as much as a year, cancellation of insurance coverage, mandatory jail sentences. If you have knowlege about laws in your state, your arguments will be much more convincing.

Find out what your children think about car games such as racing on back roads with lights out; chicken – where two youthful drivers speed their cars at one another on a collision course until one of them swerves to avoid a head-on; spinning – speeding and then slamming on the brakes to send the automobile into a 180 degree spin; scrunching – piling four or five teenagers or more into the front seat while the car is operated at high speed; and sex play – where a speeding driver is enticed by his female companion until he becomes distracted and has to slow down. Dangerous as these games are at any time, they can be even more of a death trap when drugs are being used by the participants.

Find out what your children think about someone who drinks a lot and still drives. What do they think about the maturity of such an individual. Discuss this attitude and consider some of the ways a responsible person can "prove himself or herself" to friends and family.

Always keep lines of communication open. This means that you should be free and easy to talking to your children about all kinds of subjects and that you don't just start conversations with them to give dire warning. Make sure that your teenagers know that you consider their safety much more important than getting the family car back into the garage without a scratch. Make it clear that as far as you are concerned, no conceivable situation could ever justify driving after drinking or use of other drugs.

Don't ask for perfection. Most teenagers do drink on some occasions and may either drink and drive, smoke pot and drive or are passengers in the cars of friends who do. To forbid drug activities entirely for your teenagers is almost certain to lead to breaking the rule by drinking or using drugs in secret or other problems. A far better way is to help your teenager find ways to avoid combining drugs and driving. When your teenager has acted in a responsible way in a difficult spot, be quick to show your approval and appreciation. Such a response may go a long way in giving the youth confidence to resist peer pressure and not "go along with the crowd" in similar situations in the future.

If you are a teenager or young adult, keep in mind that using drugs and driving can cause all kinds of difficulties, even if you do not actually get drunk or completely stoned. There are certain points you should remember that may help. It's safest, of course, not to drink or use other drugs at all. If you do drink, don't drink any faster than your body can burn up the alcohol. This means not more than one drink every two hours for the average-sized person.

Sip, don't gulp your drink, and be sure to eat something before or while you're drinking. The food in your stomach will help slow the passage of alcohol into the bloodstream and into the brain. Don't drink at all when you are in an upset state of mind. When you drink to escape problems, you are running the risk of becoming dependent upon alcohol. Don't mix drinking with other activities such as swimming and boating, because alcohol greatly increases your chances of an accident.

If you should get drunk, the one and only way to sober up is to wait until the alcohol leaves your system. Showers, hot coffee, and other so-called remedies are of no help at all in overcoming the effects of alcohol. Instead of taking the wheel, ask a friend to drive. If you're by yourself, call someone – a friend, an older brother or sister, or a parent – for a ride.

A difficult situation can develop if you are with a friend who drinks too much and still insists that driving is no problem. Even though you may feel it's easier just to keep quiet and not make trouble, this is the kind of spot where for your safety and the safety of your friends you should stir up trouble. If you're with a group, you might try to head off the problem by jointly designating one person to stay sober and drive. If this tactic doesn't work, you can offer to drive yourself or wait until your friend becomes sober. If all strategies fail and your friend is still determined to drive, don't go along on the ride. There's nothing cool or daring or loyal about riding with a drinking driver. Arrange a ride with someone else, call home for a ride, or telephone for a cab. Your parents will probably be glad to pick up the tab for the taxi if you don't have enough for the fare yourself. Remember, there's always another way to get to your destination, even if it means walking.

It can also be a tough spot if all of your friends are drinking and you are a person who does not drink at all or you do not feel like drinking at that particular time. In our drinking society, it's easy to forget that it's perfectly OK not to use alcohol and that there are many very good reasons not to drink. Some people just don't like the taste or the feeling of disorientation that alcohol often causes. Still others don't drink for religious or family reasons or perhaps because they are alcoholics and know it.

Even if you sometimes have a drink or two, there may be certain times when you just don't feel like drinking or may not want to drink because you will be driving. If you don't want to drink, don't do it. It is not easy to resist pressure from your friends, especially if you find yourself at a party that centers around a keg of beer or a bottle of wine.

One way to refuse a drink is with a simple, direct "No thanks." If one of your buddies asks, "Why not?" you can add to your response by saying, "I have to drive and I don't want to kill myself or anyone else." Such a reply is hard to dispute. Having a few facts about drinking and driving may help. You may find that others in the group will admire your stand and join in supporting you in not wanting to drink.

An important fact to keep in mind is that nobody can "get you drunk." Someone may try, but in the end, it's your decision, because it's you who is in control. If someone tries to pressure you to have a drink you don't want, the simple "No thanks" or "I've had enough" is usually all that's needed. State your refusal pleasantly, but in a positive way so that there is no question in anybody's mind about what you mean. Say no in any way you please.

In a television commercial on ways to refuse drinks prepared for the 1982 Alcohol Abuse Prevention Campaign two men, one in his 20s and the other in his 30s, are arm wrestling at a table in a bar as a number of patrons look on. With his right arm the younger man forces his opponent's right arm to the table and wins the contest as the onlookers applaud. The older man asks the younger man his name.

"People call me Lefty!" he replies. The older man looks incredulous then suggests a drink and another match.

"I'm quittin'," Lefty replies. "You're quittin'?" the older man asks.

"I'm quittin' . . . drinkin'," Lefty replies.

On the highway, many of us have had the frightening experience of driving near a driver under the influence of alcohol or other drug. The erratic behavior of such a driver includes weaving from side to side, endangering himself and others on the road. The driver under the influence may be difficult to spot in some cases. Possible indications of such a driver include the following:

Unreasonably high speed
Unreasonably low speed
Hugging the center line or driving with two wheels off the pavement or bumping along the curb
Spurts of fast and slow driving
Cutting in sharply ahead of a car after passing a car
Driving without lights at night
Changing lanes for no apparent reason
Ignoring traffic signs
Failing to respond to normal driving courtesies such as dimming lights and yielding on merging roads
Approaching traffic controls too fast or too slow
Driving in the wrong gear
Driving with windows open in cold weather
Driving with head protruding from the window

Of course, if you suspect that another driver is under the influence, you should put as much distance between your vehicle and his as possible. You should also note the license number and report it to the state police as soon as you can so that others on the highway can be protected.

Since the effects of alcohol are both psychological and physiological, and the psychological effects show up first, some people retain a surprising degree of driving skill even under the influence of alcohol. Despite the adeptness they may show, their driving judgement is greatly impaired. This is an excellent reason why you should learn to drive defensively, if you are not already doing so; by defensive driving, you can protect your life and those of your passengers.

If, by any chance, you are the driver under the influence of drugs, get off the highway at once to avoid the appointment with tragedy that drugs and driving may be arranging for you and your passengers.

So far, we have been talking mainly about what individuals as party hosts, parents, or youths can do to help in prevention efforts. In dealing with the problem of drugs and driving, a number of communities such as Philadelphia and Pittsburgh have developed Alcohol Highway Safety Programs (AHSP) for people who have been involved in Driving Under the Influence (DUI) episodes. These programs furnish alternatives such as counseling and education to the usual penalties for drinking and driving. For information about programs of this kind in your community, contact your state agency listed in Chapter 12.

On a national level, the SOBER campaign, Slow on the Bottle, Enjoy the Road, is an effort to bring home the message that drinking and driving can have tragic results. In 1973 the National Council on Alcoholism, Delaware Valley Area, Inc., the Philadelphia Safe Driving Program, and the Philadelphia Jaycees joined forces in a public information campaign aimed at promoting public awareness about the dangers of drinking and driving. An advertising agency contributed its services to create the slogan and logo, SOBER. The slogan and picture of the overturned car provided the spark that caught the interest of the mass media and the public to such an extent that the campaign has now been adopted in 35 states.

Figure 17. The SOBER campaign is one of a number of efforts to combat alcohol-related highway accidents.

Still another national program is Driving While Intoxicated Counterattack. Recognizing that traditional punitive measures have not succeeded, DWI Counterattack offers instead an educational program for persons convicted of driving while intoxicated – a program that can be organized by a concerned civic group in any community with the assistance of the American Automobile Association (AAA) Club Assistance.

AAA Club DWI Schools give accurate information to drivers about alcohol's effects on their driving performance and help them to assess their own drinking and driving behavior. The goal is to develop personal plans to avoid future DWI arrests and make highways safer for everyone.

Chapter 9

DRUG HIGHS VERSUS NATURAL HIGHS

THERE is just no denying that for many people, drug highs give a great number of pleasures. Drug users report that colors are brighter, sounds are louder and clearer, and highs are accompanied by feelings of elation, exhilaration, a sense of "floating in the air," relaxation, and happiness. However, these highs eventually come to an end, and what price does the drug user pay for them? Following many drug highs there is a sickening plunge into an environment of despair, humiliation, hopelessness, isolation, nervousness, and depression – depression that is sometimes so deep that it leads to thoughts of suicide and in not a few cases the actual taking of a life. Sometimes the life of a youth who has just started to live is forfeited.

Drug highs can have other particularly grisly effects not only for the drug abuser but also for others with whom he comes in contact. One man who reported having been on a PCP high committed a ghastly mutilation murder during which he tore out the eyeballs of his victim, a woman. He now faces a trial and a possible sentence of death or life imprisonment. Of course, he can never undo his act performed while under the effect of a drug, and this he must live with, however long his life lasts.

In addition to senseless effects on mental and emotional health, drug highs have devastating physical effects. These can include vomiting, diarrhea, constipation, pains and aching, and amnesia. Recently, as we describe in another chapter, it was found that a certain drug can lead to fungal infections. Just about everyone is familiar with the results of the hangover from drinking too much alcohol. If they have not experienced it themselves, they know people who have. A head sensitive to the touch and even the slightest movement, upset stomach, dejection, guilt, and embarassment all too often follow a heavy bout of drinking. That little or nothing may be recalled from the episode can only add to the anxiety that results from it. The individual can be shaken by doubts about what was actually said or what physical harm he or she may have caused, particularly if an automobile was driven during the blackout and the auto shows any signs of recent damage such as a cracked headlight or dented fender. The descent from a drug high is usually abrupt and complete, leaving the drug user in a state of trauma.

A girl in her early 20s borrowed her father's car to go to a party. After the party, at which she got high on alcohol, she climbed into the automobile and started to drive home, not realizing that the car had a flat tire. The damaged tire was soon reduced to ribbons, and the car bumped along on the bare metal of the wheel as she continued to drive in a black-out condition. Oblivious to the sparks flying from beneath the car as the vehicle, sagging to one side, scraped along the roadway, she drove on until she reached her home.

An examination of the auto the next day revealed damages of more than $1,000, which included a twisted main frame. Even with this outlay of money, the mechanics found themselves unable to restore quite the proper camber to the front wheels, making it unsafe to drive without further expensive repairs. The family eventually sold the car. Traumatic as the situation was for the girl the morning following the party as she descended quickly from the high of the previous night, things could have been far worse if she had hit a pedestrian or had collided with another automobile.

A high from drinking beer apparently played a part in a fatal boating accident at a lake in Eastern Pennsylvania. A boat that was turned too abruptly by the operator capsized, throwing him and two other men into 40-degree water. The men clung to the overturned boat and life jackets they had not worn. They pushed the boat toward the shore, but the anchor hit bottom and they couldn't move it any farther. One man was able to swim to shore.

The two who stayed with the boat finally lost consciousness in the chilling water and slipped beneath the surface.

A patrolman investigating the accident said he had been told by the survivor that the boaters had drunk "three or four" cans of beer before launching the boat.

"It may have affected their thinking," the patrolman said. "Like drinking and driving, drinking and operating a boat don't mix." He also said that hypothermia, a lowering of body temperature, probably was a factor in the two deaths.

Not only can drug highs lead to the kind of accidents we have described they can also lead to fatalities from overdosing.

Let's think now about some natural highs. As the Pennsylvania Governor's Council on Drug and Alcohol Abuse points out, "Doing something for yourself can mean a lot to someone else." Natural highs can come from something you do for yourself as well as something you do for someone else.

The Governor's Council made these suggestions: If you have time on your hands you can put it to good use to do something for other people. You may be surprised at the number of things you can do for free and that will give you a natual high. Improvise and be creative, because in finding joy in people you like, you can find joy in yourself.

You might organize a sports day and invite everyone on the block – mothers, grandparents, and kids. Pack a picnic and choose up sides. Then spend the day in the local park, running relays and three-legged races, throwing frisbees, playing baseball, and team charades.

You might think up a new game, the Council suggests. Games are fun but they can even be more fun to think them up than they are to play. Get the neighborhood kids together and invent a new game.

How about a club? Whatever kids do, it's more fun with two. Help in organizing a club. Maybe even a club just to meet and carry out activities like the ones we have been discussing.

A club house goes along with the idea of a club. You can go all the way with two-by-fours, plywood, nails and hinges or you can create with boxes and crates. Kids love to have their own private place, because it's something special for them.

Another idea from the Council is to put on a show. You can stage a play or a series of plays. The libraries are full of plays for children. They're tremendous fun to put on and to watch. You can start your own neighborhood repertory company.

Developing a Pen Pal Program is yet another idea the Council suggests. Nothing brings rewards in quite the same way as a letter from a far-off place. You can help youngsters in the neighborhood to have pen pals across the country or even halfway around the world in such places as Australia and New Guinea.

If there's a plot of ground in your neighborhood, you might start a neighborhood garden. You can plant flowers, bushes, or even trees, or you can raise vegetables. In these days of high inflation, we all know that money doesn't grow in trees, but peaches do, the Council points out.

As far as your own family is concerned, you can turn the family into a team and really clean your home from top to bottom. Organize it as a game or jump in and adopt it as a project.

There's something about getting rid of a lot of old items like newspapers and broken furniture that can give you a real feeling of accomplishment. Hold a garage sale and use the money to do something you really enjoy.

Living with the stars on a clear night can touch us all. An inexpensive telescope can enable you and your friends to study the moon and the stars. A shooting star can give a natural high that can last for days and can make your spirits soar.

Few natural highs can match that of painting pictures in oils, acrylics, or just plain inexpensive transparent water colors that come in the small metal box. The painter experiences many highs in the painting of just one picture. Finding just the right scene or still life that combines color and composition is always a thrill for the painter. He looks over the scene from several different angles, finally finding the perspective that suits him best. Laying out the picture with charcoal or pencil on paper or canvas is also exciting, but the high reaches its peak when with the application of color the picture unfolds, whether a landscape, still life, or portrait.

If you like to draw or paint, sharpen your skills. Try your hand at preparing a picture that is good enough to give to a friend or a relative as a gift or perhaps even of such quality that it can be entered in competition at an art exhibition. Once you have painted a picture that you are really proud of, you will find yourself on a high that can last for days. Your feeling is, "I can really paint well when I put my mind and talents to it."

If painting isn't to your particular liking, there are crafts you can get into such as latch hooking. Or you might try collecting things. There are so many items to be collected such as comic books, baseball cards, and even clothes irons. There is just no end to the possibilities.

Playing a musical instrument affords fine possibilities for natural highs. One 21 year old we know is so hooked on playing the piano that it is the first thing he does in the morning and the last thing at night. Try organizing a combo of musicians in your neighborhood. Find a location where your rehearsals won't drive the neighbors up a wall. Copy the style of one of your favorite groups or develop one of your own and see how far your band can go. You might start by playing in some parties. Even the Beach Boys had to start someplace.

Natural highs abound in athletics. The quarterback who sends a touchdown pass spiraling into the arms of a receiver, the hitter who connects with a solid double to score a teammate, the basketball player who scores a field goal to give this team a victory are all feeling the exhilaration of natural highs. More and more girls are getting into athletics, and girls are proving they can rival boys in spirit and ability.

Even professional athletes who have been competing in their favorite sports for years have repeated natural highs. Tug McGraw of the Phillies pounds his glove and dances a jig from the mound when he strikes out the last batter.

McGraw, probably the most sought after of all the 1980 World Champion Phillies for public appearances, has had many natural highs as a result of his performance in the World Series that year. These include his recitations of "Casey at the Bat" at such locations as the Academy of Music in Philadelphia and at luncheons, awards dinners, and other special occasions. In each of his appearances, he strives to outdo his previous efforts.

Natural highs are often frequently experienced by college

Figure 18. A sport such as football provides many opportunities for natural highs.

players such as James Worthy, the All-American forward at the University of North Carolina, who probably experienced the greatest natural high of his sports career when his team won the 1982 NCAA National Basketball Championship. He celebrated the victory over Georgetown by cutting the net from the basket seconds after the game ended, while 60,000 fans applauded in the Superdome.

We certainly don't want to give the impression that a person has to be a top athlete to have natural highs from sports. These highs are just as real and thrilling whether they are experienced at the Superdome before 60,000 fans or at a sandlot, rec center, or tennis court down the block from your home with only a handful of your fellow players at hand.

Of course, there are just all kinds of opportunities offering possibilities for natural highs. Three young boys who were neighbors, at the suggestion of the mother of one of the boys, began planning a hike along the Applachian Trail, which meanders through mountains, valleys, and hills more than 2,000 miles from Georgia to Maine. During many cold winter evenings the boys poured over maps, laid out routes along a section of the trail extending through Pennsylvania, and planned meals and stopovers at shelters scattered along the trail. When warm weather finally arrived, the boys put their plans into action, and the result was a natural high that lasted not only for the week's trip but also for long afterward.

Figure 19. Backpacking furnishes a natural high that can be enjoyed by youths as well as adults.

One of the boys became so enamoured with traveling during the trek that over the next few years he launched a whole series of trips, some of his own and some with companions, which took him to such far away places as Japan, Afghanistan, Nepal, Thailand, Pakistan, and India. In Japan, he met a small dark-haired girl from Italy whom he later married and with whom he is now continuing his travels. The enjoyment that he is gaining from these trips, supplemented by a diary and a photographic record, will very likely give him natural highs for years to come as he relives his many adventures and perhaps writes articles about them.

Many youths have highs from religious experiences in which they find a special closeness to God, develop increased faith, and are spiritually united with people of the same beliefs. Through their religious experiences, they not only benefit personally but also often help others less fortunate than themselves.

Of course, there are lots of other ways to have natural highs – whitewater boating, water skiing, mountain climbing, and piloting a plane. These are not for you, you may say, because of their cost or difficulty in getting to locations where they can be enjoyed. Consider for a moment some of the other possibilities for highs that are within the reach of almost everyone, such as jogging, camping, biking, dancing, swimming, and just plain brisk hiking.

Scuba diving has lots of possibilities, and you don't have to travel to Hawaii to do it. It's a bit risky, but it can provide a lot of thrills. Spelunking or exploring caves is still another way to get a natural high, and as long as you are a bit cautious, it can be a thrilling experience and one that can be enjoyed in many parts of the country.

There's no doubt that natural highs have many advantages over drug highs. For one thing, you don't have that devastating let down feeling that follows a drug high. True, no one can stay on cloud nine forever, and let downs will in time follow natural highs, whatever their nature. However, these quite mild effects can't be compared to the crushing psychological and physiological reactions from drug highs, which sometimes bring people to the brink of suicide and in some cases catapult them over the edge.

Natural highs often build on themselves to bring even greater satisfactions. The artist or musician who, prompted by the highs she experiences, work to become even more skilled and finds the quality of her performance improves. The baseball outfielder who revels in chasing down towering fly balls spends hours practicing catches of all kinds until he becomes even better at his position.

Drug highs and their abrupt let down drain a person emotionally and physically and leave the drug abuser in a condition where greater quantities of a particular drug are often needed to produce the same results. On the other hand, natural highs in most cases combine to make the individual a happier, more satisfied, more productive, and more complete person.

Chapter 10

DRUGS AND THE LAW

THE death of a young girl, struck from behind by a hit-and-run driver, has led to tougher drunk driving laws in her home state and increased concern about ways of dealing with drunken drivers in many parts of the nation. The girl, Cari Lightner, was killed as she walked to a church carnival in her hometown of Fair Oaks, California. It turned out that the driver of the car was a 47-year-old man with two prior drunk driving convictions who was out on bail on a third arrest and who previously had spent just two days in jail. Apparently he had never been treated for his drinking.

As a result of this tragic accident, the girl's mother, Candi Lightner, established Mothers Against Drunk Drivers (MADD) and started a personal campaign aimed at strengthening laws concerning people who drive under the influence. Mrs. Lightner now appears on television and radio programs and testifies at hearings on legislation. Local communities are forming MADD organizations to promote the goals of the group, and in just two years, MADD has grown to 83 chapters in 29 states. California is one of a number of states that have passed tougher drunk driving laws.

The purpose of this chapter on drugs and the law is not only to provide a brief review of certain legislation already in effect but also to give information about new laws that may soon be implemented.

Since the early 1900s, the automobile has progressed from a slow, unreliable method of transportation to the preferred means of travel for most people, particularly in the United States. Fast, comfortable, and quite inexpensive compared to other modes of travel, the automobile is used by people of all ages. It is especially favored by teenagers and young adults, who place owning an automobile high on their list of priorities.

At the same time that the popularity of the automobile has grown in its 80 years, it has become one of the most lethal objects known to man. In any given year, it has exacted a greater toll on the American public than any recent wars. In the last 10 years of the war in Vietnam, there were 45,000 United States fatalities, yet in the year 1982 alone, there were 52,000 deaths on the nation's highways. Among the striking aspects of these fatalities are not only the high number of deaths among auto passengers compared with drivers but also that just about half of the fatalities are alcohol related.

In a recent editorial in *Alcoholism,* Jerauld D. Miller, publisher, wrote that America's answer to highway deaths, unscientific as it may be, will likely come on a state by-state basis. It appears that this will be accomplished as a great number of local laws, lobbies, and legislatures stress enforcement, sentencing, and punishment.

In the face of increasing public pressure, many states have rushed new provisions into law that contain various penalties. Utah enacted what was termed "the toughest law," only to have Colorado follow only days later with even stricter legislation. Already this year (1982) 27 states have passed their version of tough drunk driving legislation. Reversing a trend toward lower drinking ages, 20 states have raised the legal drinking age. The lowered drinking ages made alcohol-related crashes by far the greatest killer of Americans between the ages of 16 and 24. After New Jersey lowered its drinking age to 18, the average number of persons killed annually by 18-to-20-year-old drivers in that state climbed by 176 percent.

Helping to trigger the new rash of strict laws, in addition to MADD, is an organization that developed in New York State, Remove Intoxicated Drivers. (RID). RID now lists 55 chapters in 29 states. According to an article in *Newsweek*, energy for the new campaigns against driving under the influence also originates among officials who have suffered personal tragedies such as State Senator William Smith of New York, whose daughter was killed in a head-on collision with a drunk driver. Senator Smith was responsible for writing one of the three laws to control drunken driving passed in his state in 1980.

Partly in response to the death of State Representative Clare Dunn, who was killed by a driver under the influence driving on the wrong side of the highway, the legislature of Arizona began the consideration of new laws. Charlotte Kitowsky, a registered nurse in Connecticut, started a get tough lobbying campaign after she almost lost her life to a drunken driver. Sometime after the accident, she learned jail charges against him were dropped and the episode expunged from his record.

A bill that will stiffen the penalties for persons convicted of drunken driving in Pennsylvania was recently signed into law by Governor Dick Thornburgh. Under the bill, first-time drunken driving offenders will face a minimum 48-hour imprisonment or acceptance into the state's Accelerated Rehabilitative Disposition Program instead of the probation that first offenders now tend to receive. A person convicted of killing someone in a drunken driving accident will serve no less than three years in prison compared with the maximum five-year term and $10,000 fine now in effect.

A campaign against drunk driving is currently underway in the state of Maine. Posters mounted in prominent locations throughout the state point out that penalties for drunk driving are severe. When criminally convicted, even a first offender gets a minimum of two days in jail, a fine of $350, and a loss of license for 90 days. The Maine Safety Committee stresses in the posters that drunken driving is not worth the gamble. The campaign uses a logo showing a diagonal slash through the drawing of a driver under the influence.

The new laws and special campaigns reveal a hard-line approach to drunk drivers, who, in addition to causing about 26,000 deaths annually and hundreds of thousands of costly accidents, are responsible for many injuries that handicap people for life. In 1981, the state of Maryland, reacting to the toll of deaths and injuries, created a special state police unit to identify drunk drivers. The effort included setting up roadblocks on a number of the state's highways, resulting in a doubling of arrests for drivers under the influence.

Three major points are made by most of the new laws. The first is that a blood alcohol content of .10 (three beers or glasses of wine or two shot glasses of whiskey consumed in one hour by a 160-pound man) constitutes a crime by itself. Previously, such consumption was considered merely as evidence against the person. Also, many of the new laws make prison mandatory, if not for the first offense, certainly for the second. In addition, they often increase penalties for drivers who refuse the blood alcohol test and require that all convictions, regardless of how the court disposes of them, be listed on a driver's record.

Only a few of the new state laws recognize that the alcoholic person driving under the influence is a special kind of offender who requires thoughtful management. More than 54 percent of all people who are arrested for the first time driving under the influence are problem drinkers. This is not because alcoholics drive more than nonalcoholics, but because they are more often under the influence of alcohol when they do drive. Because more than 70 percent of second offenders and nearly 100 percent of individuals who are arrested for the third time for driving under the influence are alcoholics, the first frightening and threatening experience has not changed their behavior. For most of the others, who are primarily social drinkers, the first shocking experience is usually enough to convince them never to drive while under the influence. This makes it clear that it is the disease of alcoholism, not law breaking or antisocial behavior, that must be dealt with.

In a recent edition of the *CODAAP Report,* a publication of the Philadelphia Department of Public Health, the Habitual Alcohol Drunk Drivers Program (HADD) was described. In this project, the department's Coordinating Office for Drug and Alcohol Abuse Programs (CODAAP) in cooperation with the city's Adult Probation Department and the court system is launching a new program for those persons found guilty of more than one drunken driving offense. This new effort involves an intensive treatment program using inpatient and outpatient therapy suited to the individual needs of the offender. This is only one of several programs in which CODAAP is engaged that stress alcohol education and information along with treatment of the problem drinker-driver.

As might be expected, there has been criticism of the new drinking and driving laws. Some local communities maintain that they do not have adequate funding to carry out the new legislation. Certain critics contend that the new laws by themselves are not sufficient to reduce the death and injury toll. Albert Kramer, a Massachusetts judge, says that jails are not enough and that imprisonment should be combined with intensive rehabilitation.

His ideas coincide to some extent with programs underway in certain communities. Prior to 1972, the courts ordinarily used only such measures as fines and jail sentences in dealing with drunken drivers. In that year, the National Alcohol Highway Safety Program was established which emphasizes education and information programs as part of rehabilitation rather than depending entirely upon the traditional punitive sanctions.

Since that program was instituted, in the city of Philadelphia alone, more than 21,000 persons have been involved in the Alcohol Highway Safety Program. In one recent year in Philadelphia, there were 4,662 arrests for driving under the influence, and more than 1,600 traffic accidents were caused by drivers who had been drinking. Of those arrested, approximately 3,000 individuals were diverted to the Alcohol Highway Safety Program, and 1,341 were placed in treatment.

The federal government proposes a three-year, $125 million program of incentive grants to states. Grants would be made to states that rank highest in a six-point campaign including the following elements: better enforcement of laws supported by public information, a statewide system of keeping track of repeat offenders, and the presumption that a person is driving while under the influence if the blood alcohol level (BAL) is .10. The point system would include suspension of driving licenses or permits, a screening of alcohol-related behavior before sentences are meted out, the court sanctions for persons driving under the influence. Among the court sanctions would be such aspects as community service, fines, imprisonment, and, in addition to alcohol safety education programs, some form of treatment.

As Jerauld Miller points out in his editorial, the drunken driving problem cannot be solved without four vital elements – Prevention, Penalty, Protection, and Rehabilitation. The authors agree with Miller's emphasis of the following: If the goal to reduce driving deaths dramatically isn't enough incentive, Drinking Under the Influence programs (DUI) should be considered as a quick and effective way of helping problem drinkers. Among the national population of millions of alcoholics, no more than 15 percent will seek treatment on their own, with perhaps a million being successful in their quest for treatment and recovery. However, if America were to declare an unlimited war on drunk drivers, handing out mandatory treatment for the 700,000 alcoholics convicted of DUI each year, the number of recovered alcoholics could be greatly increased.

The recovery of alcoholics not only alleviates the drinking and driving problem but also lessens other difficulties in the community that arise from alcohol abuse. As far as laws regarding drinking in general are concerned, most American jurisdictions attempt to regulate drinking through the criminal law. Since the consumption of alcohol is usually legal and the use of alcohol is socially accepted and approved, the law tries to deal with certain parts of the problem of excessive drinking.

In the past, the main aim of the law has been concern for the peace and quiet of the community rather than the welfare of the drinker. As a result, the major effect of the criminal law in controlling drinking behavior usually deals with only a small group of public drinkers. These individuals who become offensive because of their noise and other antisocial actions, including threats to other people, attacks upon them, and damage to property.

Even when bodily assault takes place, no legal action usually results unless the attack is witnessed by a police officer or the victim is willing to obtain an arrest warrant for the assailant and follow up with action through the courts. In many cases, the victim of the assault is unwilling to go through the necessary legal procedures, and the offender is not prosecuted. As one official in the alcohol field put it recently, enforcement of local laws dealing with public drinking is lukewarm at best.

A number of sections of the criminal law have traditionally concerned drinking. The mildest of these, which still may be found in certain jurisdictions, is prohibition of drinking in public. In some cases, the states specify particular places in public where drinking is prohibited such as churches, public meeting halls, wharves, trains, or even in one instance athletic events conducted by schools. The offense of public drinking is usually not prosecuted when a more serious charge may be brought. Until recently, in at least one state, however, a person who took a swallow from a flask at a school athletic contest could be cited for committing a misdemeanor punishable by up to 60 days in prison.

The person who consumes alcohol in public is more likely to be arrested for being publicly intoxicated. In most of the communities that still retain the offense, the charge of public intoxication can be proved by showing that the defendant was in a public place and acted as if he were drunk in such ways as loud, garbled speech, swaying gait, or slovenly appearance.

Another offense that is found on the statute books of a number of states is that of drunk and disorderly conduct, which is usually regarded as a more serious offense than public intoxication. The penalties accorded for each of these offenses are still quite similar, however, ranging in the several states from a fine of a few dollars to as much as $1,000 or jail terms ranging from a few days to one year. Typically, the range of penalties is from $25 to $300 and from 30 days to three months. Actually, the fines imposed by the criminal courts are likely to be minimal, and the jail terms given are apt to be only for a few days. These light sanctions are given even though the jurisdictions may have laws that provide for much heavier penalties.

Vagrancy is another class of criminal conduct that is used in some places to control drinking in public. A number of vagrancy statutes define the vagrant as a person who is a "common drunkard" or "habitual drunkard." It seems, however, that prosecutions on the charge of vagrancy are losing their popularity and may eventually disappear from the statute books. In large cities today, people in various stages of drunkenness are common sights on streets and in doorways.

In the various states, a great variety of methods are employed in legislation to control drinking. In some cases, there is prohibition of the consumption of alcohol in public places, except for those locations having licensed permits. Legislation often specifies that sales to intoxicated or disorderly persons are unlawful and that it is a violation for a licensee to allow such a person to stay on the premises. In one midwestern state, for example, legislation specifies that it is unlawful to sell liquor to persons under legal age, intoxicated individuals, habitual drunkards or spendthrifts or other persons who are insane, mentally deficient, or in need of medical treatment.

Violation of state law regarding services to underage, intoxicated persons or certain other individuals may result in stiff penalties: a fine of $500 or a jail sentence of six months for a first offense. For a second offense, the law may call for a $1,000 fine and a one-year sentence.

Efforts to control drinking may be attempted through the types of liquor licenses awarded. Retail licenses may constitute a number of general types such as liquor store, liquor-licensed drugstore, hotel and restaurant, and club. A facility licensed as a retail liquor store may sell beverages in sealed containers only for drinking off the premises. Licensed drugstores may sell liquor only in the original containers for off-premises consumption, while only liquor stores and drugstores are authorized to sell liquor by the bottle. A hotel and restaurant license furnishes the authorization for sales of liquor by the drink, but drinks may be served only with meals. Club licenses may also be procured that authorize sales by the drink, although such sales may be made only to members of the particular club and their guests.

Another way that the control of liquor is attempted is through the prohibition of liquor sales at certain times. For example, sales may be prohibited from 2 AM to 7 AM on weekdays and from 1 AM on Sunday until 7 AM the following Monday. In one southern state where such hours are in effect, all counties are dry until there is an affirmative vote for the establishment of "county liquor control stores." The law in this state also specifies that sales to persons under the age 21 are unlawful, but the law allows a minor to drink in the privacy of his own home with the permission of his parents. In most states, legal drinking age applies only to drinking in public places, but some states include private homes under this provision. Legal drinking age ranges in the various states from 18 to 21 years. Somc state laws call for the prohibition of sales on election days and on Christmas day. Another approach used in some cases is to limit the number of licensed premises to one for each specific number of residents of the state, such as one license for each 2,000 inhabitants.

A number of states have maintained tight controls regarding the transportation of liquor in motor vehicles. In at least one such state, such regulations specify that only one gallon can be transported in any one vehicle at any time, and all open bottles must be kept outside the passenger area. This has the effect of requiring the carrying of such beverages only in the trunk.

The wording of the regulations is usually phrased along these lines: "No person shall transport, carry, possess or have any alcoholic beverage in or upon any motor vehicle except in the original package with the seal unbroken." The penalties for infractions may range up to $500. If enforced, such regulations discourage people from having an open bottle in a car. Travelers usually dispose of or leave a partly consumed bottle of expensive whiskey rather than take the chance of the imposition of a stiff fine. In at least one state, however, it was found that youths drinking at a supper club would finish off a bottle rather than leave it half filled. The state law now allows an open bottle in a motor vehicle if not located in the passenger area.

One way of determining the effectiveness of alcohol beverage laws in the various states is to find out whether there is any relationship between the laws of a certain jurisdiction and the per capita consumption of liquor of the people residing in that jurisdiction. States that have government-owned liquor stores are termed control states. States having privately owned liquor stores are termed license states. According to the book *Drinking – Alcohol in American Society – Issues and Current Research,* those states with privately owned liquor stores tend to have a higher per capita consumption than those with government-owned stores.

The book also points out that per capita liquor consumption is likely to be greater in states with a high ratio of liquor outlets to total population, and states without liquor-by-the-drink establishments tend to have lower consumption level than those with liquor by the drink. Late closing hours for liquor outlets and lowering of age requirements for buying hard liquor also tend to increase per capita consumption.

Recently, laws in some states have placed less emphasis on punishing alcohol abusers and more on giving opportunities for treatment.

Efforts to control drugs other than alcohol are handled in a different and somewhat more coordinated manner. The 1970 Controlled Substances Act of the federal government designates a listing of "controlled drugs" and places them on a schedule or in special categories to prevent, curtail, and limit them. Under the Controlled Substances Act, the Attorney General of the United States, on recommendation of the Secretary of the Department of Health, Education and Welfare, now the Department of Health and Human Services, was given certain authority in dealing with drugs.

This authority consisted of placing drugs in five schedules or categories, based on their relative potential for abuse, scientific evidence of the drug's pharmacological effects, the state of current scientific knowledge about the drug, and its history and current pattern of abuse. The five schedules have different penalties for violations with Schedule I being designated the heaviest and Schedule V the mildest. Among the drugs that are controlled are the opiates, amphetamines, hallucinogens, marijuana, and depressants. Detailed information about drugs listed in each schedule is available from the National Clearinghouse on Drug Abuse Information listed in Chapter 12.

Schedule I substances are drugs that have no accepted medical use in the United States and have a high potential for drug abuse. Examples of drugs in this schedule include heroin, LSD, peyote, mescaline and psilocybin. Drugs included under Schedule II substances have a high abuse potential and also are very likely to result in psychological or physical dependence. Substances in this category consist of certain narcotic drugs and drugs containing amphetamines or methamphetamines as the single active ingredient or in combination with each other. Examples are opium, cocaine, methadone, and a unadulterated amphetamines or methamphetamines. Other examples are amobarbital, pentobarbital, secobarbital and methaqualone. Drugs in Schedule III have an abuse potential less than those in Schedule I and II. This schedule covers compounds containing limited quantities of certain narcotics and nonnarcotic drugs. Examples are derivatives of barbituric acid. Paragoric is also included in the schedule.

Schedule IV substances include such drugs as barbital and phenobarbital. These are drugs that have a smaller abuse potential than drugs in Schedule III.

Drugs listed in Schedule V have still a smaller abuse potential. The preparations listed under this schedule contain certain moderate, limited quantities of narcotic drugs, generally those used for treatment of coughs and diarrhea, which may be distributed without a prescription order. Enforcement of the Controlled Substances Act is the responsibility of the Drug Enforcement Administration (DEA) of the U.S. Department of Justice.

Separate laws relating to the distribution of controlled substances have been enacted in most states. In many cases, state law is much more stringent than federal law. Because of the different ways in which drug offenders and offenses are handled in the 50 states, there is need for increased public knowledge about laws in the states. A considerable amount of uniformity exists, however, because certain states have adopted the federal Controlled Substances act. Guidelines prepared cooperatively by the DEA and the DEA Practitioners Working Committee provide an example of good practices that should be encouraged under both federal and state laws and regulations. Close cooperation and understanding between law enforcement and medicine help to insure that legitimate drugs remain in legitimate channels.

Medical doctors who prescribe controlled drugs have the responsibility to inform patients of the effects of prescribed drugs in accordance with medical practice and professional judgement. Correspondingly, the patient has the duty to follow the directions of the prescriber for the use of the medicine.

The most common and well-known method for controlling drug traffic is criminal sanctions. Under the Controlled Substances Act, trafficking is defined as the unauthorized manufacture, distribution, or possession with the intent to distribute any controlled substance. Distribution is considered to be delivery whether by sale, as a gift, or in any other manner.

Most drug offenders are prosecuted under state laws. You may find that the laws in your state are even more strict than the federal laws. According to present terms of the federal Controlled Substances Act, penalties for unlawful possession for a first offense are up to one year imprisonment and/or fines up to $5,000. For a second offense, the punishment is twice the penalty imposed for the first offense.

A first offender who is under 21 may have the official record of arrest, trial, and conviction erased upon satisfactory completion of probation.

Laws for unlawful distribution or possession with intent to distribute are even more severe. For narcotics, such laws call for up to 15 years imprisonment and/or fines up to $25,000 plus a mandatory 3-year special parole for a first offense. For a second offense, the punishment is up to twice the penalties for the first offense.

Unlawful distribution or possession with intent to distribute in regard to other drugs has the following penalties: For a first offense, the punishment is up to five years imprisonment and/or fines up to $15,000. In addition, there is a mandatory two-year special parole. Punishment for a second offense is up to twice the penalties for the first offense.

A person more than 18 years of age who unlawfully distributes drugs to a youth under 21 is punished for a first offense by up to twice the penalties otherwise authorized. For a second offense of this kind, the penalties are up to three times the penalties otherwise authorized.

Anyone who takes part in continuing criminal enterprise in regard to drugs risks punishment of 10 years to life imprisonment, a fine of up to $100,000, and forfeit of profit from the enterprise. No parole is permitted. For a second offense, the punishment is 20 years to life, a fine of up to $200,000 and forfeit of profit from the enterprise. Again, no parole is allowed.

Still another habit relating to drugs and the law is the smoking of cigarettes, pipes, and cigars. More than 80 states and 100 local jurisdictions throughout the nation now have ordinances restricting smoking to designated areas in public places. In other communities, a piecemeal approach is often used with separate pieces of legislation designed to prohibit smoking in certain locations. For example, such legislation is often adopted to prohibit smoking in elevators, sports arenas, supermarkets, buses, trains, and public waiting places and hospital rooms. In instances where legislation prohibiting smoking in such locations is in effect, fines are often low–in the $10 to $25 range – and enforcement is erratic if it occurs at all. In one large city, for example, the penalty for smoking on a bus includes both a small fine and the possibility of a jail sentence. In the several years that the legislation has been in effect, however, there have been only a handful of cases in which prosecution has even been attempted.

In one eastern state where a piecemeal approach has been underway for several years, a bill was passed in 1977 prohibiting smoking in patients' rooms in hospitals. The legislation states that no person shall smoke tobacco or any other substance in a hospital patient care area or in a patient room designated as a nonsmoking room by the hospital administrator. The law also specifies that at admission to a hospital a patient may choose either a nonsmoking or smoking room and that if the type of room selected is available the patient will be placed in it. Violation of the nonsmoking provisions is punishable by a fine of $10 and costs of prosecution.

A 1978 survey of adults showed that the majority of people favored segregated smoking in trains; buses; depots, stations, and airports; theaters; eating places; indoor sporting events; public meetings; workplaces; and barbershops. Efforts are growing to limit smoking through comprehensive legislation in jurisdictions that do not have such laws on the books at the present time.

In Pennsylvania, for example, Dr. Donald Reid, Executive Secretary for Public Health, State Health Department, testified in favor of a proposal to regulate smoking in public places. The hearing was held early in 1982 at a subcommittee meeting of the state legislature.

At the hearing, Dr. Reid noted that the State Health Department supports the Clean Indoor Air Act that is under consideration by the state legislature. The act prohibits smoking in public places and at public meetings except in designated smoking areas. According to Dr. Reid, recent studies provide "strong evidence that nonsmokers who inhale smoke from a smoke-filled environment are exposed to significant health threats."

"The Health Department," Dr. Reid noted, "believes that the Clean Air Act will require minimal regulatory and cost burdens to business, since existing physical barriers and ventilation systems are to be used to minimize the effect of the smoke."

In the case of a single room open to the public, the act's provisions would be met if one side were designated nonsmoking. In addition, the provisions of the act would be waived if there were compelling reasons and the health of nonsmokers were not significantly affected. The Health Department would cooperate and coordinate actions with the Departments of Environmental Resources and Agriculture as well as with local health department in monitoring the law.

In an effort to reduce smoking among youth, the Pennsylvania Criminal Code prohibits the sale or giving of cigarettes and related paraphernalia to anyone under 16. For the first offense, the maximum fine is $25. The fine for the second offense is not to exceed $100. Third and subsequent offenses are misdemeanors.

Other controls on smoking are often directed at smoking as a public nuisance or as a fire hazard. Although smoking has not been cited as a public health hazard in certain legislation that has been passed, the overwhelming evidence citing smoking as a health hazard not only for smokers themselves but also for nonsmokers will doubtless be used increasingly as a basis for developing and supporting nonsmoking laws.

In 1974, the National Interagency Council on Smoking and Health developed a Nonsmokers Bill of Rights that includes the following statements:

Nonsmokers help to protect the health, comfort, and safety of everyone by insisting on the following rights –

THE RIGHT TO BREATHE CLEAN AIR

Nonsmokers have the right to breathe clean air, free from the harmful and irritating tobacco smoke. These rights supersede the right to smoke when the two conflict.

THE RIGHT TO SPEAK OUT

Nonsmokers have the right to express – firmly but politely – their discomfort and adverse reactions to tobacco smoke. They have the right to voice their objections when smokers light up without asking permission.

THE RIGHT TO ACT

Nonsmokers have the right to take legal action through legislative channels, social pressures or any other legitimate means – as individuals or in groups to prevent or discourage smokers from polluting the atmosphere and to seek the restriction of smoking in public places.

The third point in the "Bill of Rights" provides encouragement for those legislators, councilmen, and others who are developing legislation on the public health aspects of smoking. Such legislation has already been passed in certain communities and is being proposed in others. Despite the opposition of the Tobacco Institute and related smoking interests, it is likely that increasing numbers of local communities will be adopting legislation prohibiting smoking in public places. The presence of signs indicating nonsmoking areas tends to increase public pressure against smoking and reduce smoking in general even though official enforcement efforts may remain weak.

Federal legislation has been proposed to authorize stronger health warnings on cigarette packages. The proposed Comprehensive Smoking Prevention Act would require cigarette manufacturers to replace general health warnings on packages with specific warnings about the risk of cancer, emphysema, birth defects and heart disease. For example, the birth defects warning would state, "The Surgeon General has determined that cigarette smoking by pregnant women may result in miscarriages, premature births or child weight deficiencies."

In concluding this chapter on drugs and the law, we should like to emphasize information about identifying the drug user so that the individual can be helped through all and any means possible.

Because a drug user will do everything possible to conceal his habit, it is important to be able to recognize the outward signs and symptoms of drug abuse. One should be alert to these symptoms, but it should be realized that the drug problem is so complex that even experts sometimes have difficulty in making accurate diagnosis. The Drug Enforcement Administration (DEA) of the U.S. Department of Justice points out that it is essential not to act on your own, because it could lead to falsely accusing an innocent person. Seek professional advice and help from experts such as persons working for various agencies specializing in drug problems and also from physicians, DEA cautions.

It should always be remembered that a person may have a legitimate reason for possessing a syringe and a needle (he may be a diabetic) or having capsules and tablets (they may be prescribed by a doctor). Having the sniffles and running eyes may be due to a head cold or an allergy. Unusual or odd behavior may not be connected in any way with drug use. A good general rule for you to observe personally is *never to taste an unknown substance.*

The DEA lists the following *COMMON SIGNS OF DRUG ABUSE:*

1. Changes in attendance at work or school.
2. Change from normal capabilities (work habits, efficiency, etc.).
3. Poor physical appearance, including inattention to dress and personal hygiene.
4. Wearing sunglasses constantly at inappropriate times (indoors or at night for instance) not only to hide dilated or constricted pupils but also to compensate for the eye's inability to adjust to sunlight. Marijuana causes bloodshot eyes.
5. Unusual effort made to cover arms in order to hide needle marks.
6. Association with known drug users.
7. Stealing items which can be readily sold for cash (to support a drug habit).

INDICATIONS OF POSSIBLE MISUSE

DEPRESSANTS e.g., Quaalude, Doriden *(Barbiturates)*

A. Behavior like that of alcohol intoxication, but without the odor of alcohol on breath.

B. Staggering, stumbling, or apparent drunkenness without odor or use of alcohol.

C. Falling asleep while at work.

D. Slurred speech.

E. Pupils dilated.

F. Difficulty concentrating.

STIMULANTS *(Amphetamines)*

A. The user may be excessively active, irritable, argumentative, or nervous.

B. Excitation, euphoria, and talkativeness.

C. Pupils dilated.

D. Long periods without eating or sleeping.

E. Increased blood pressure or pulse rate.

NARCOTICS

A. Scars ("tracks") on the arms or on the backs of hands, caused by injection drugs.

B. Pupils constricted and fixed; possibly dilated during withdrawal.

C. Scratches self frequently.

D. Loss of appetite. Frequently eats candy, cookies, and drinks sweet liquids.

E. May have sniffles, red, watering eyes and a cough, which disappears when he gets a "fix." During withdrawal the addict may be nauseated and vomiting. Flushed skin, frequent yawning, and muscular twitching are common. These symptoms also disappear when the addict gets a "fix."

F. Users often leave syringes, bent spoons, cotton, needles, metal bottle caps, medicine droppers, and glassine bags in locker or desk drawers.

G. The user is lethargic, drowsy, and may go on the "nod" (i.e., an alternating cycle of dozing and awakening.)

H. Anyone dissolving tablets for injection runs a great risk and danger of lung impairment due to deposits of talcum (part of the tablet) obstructing or occluding the lung through the blood stream.

MARIJUANA

A. In the early stages of marijuana usage, the person may appear animated with rapid, loud talking and bursts of laughter. In later stages, he may be sleepy.

B. Pupils may be dilated and the eyes bloodshot.

C. May have distortions of perception and hallucinations.

The marijuana user is difficult to recognize unless he is actually under the influence of the drug, and even then, he may be able to work reasonably well. The drug may distort his depth and time perception, making driving or the operation of machinery hazardous. Long continued use of marijuana has been associated with mental deterioration.

OTHER HALLUCINOGENS

A. Behavior and mood vary widely. The user may sit or recline quietly in a trancelike state or may appear fearful or even terrified.

B. In some cases, dilated pupils.

C. Increase in blood pressure, heart rate, and blood sugar.

D. May experence nausea, chills, flushes, irregular breathing, sweating and trembling of hands.

E. There may be changes in sense of sight, hearing, touch, smell, and time.

It is unlikely that a person who uses LSD, for instance, would do so at work, since a controlled environment, often involving a friend to provide care and supervision of the user, is generally desired.

GLUE OR HYDROCARBON *(Gasoline)* SNIFFING

A. Odor of substance inhaled on breath and clothes.

B. Excessive nasal secretion and watering of the eyes.

C. Poor muscular control (staggering) within five minutes of exposure.

D. Drowsiness or unconsciousness.

E. Presence of plastic or paper bags or rags containing dry plastic cement.

F. Slurred speech.

G. Bad breath.

PHENCYCLIDINE (PCP)

Phencyclidine, developed in the 1950s, is now licitly manufactured as a veterinary anesthetic under the trade name Sernylan®. Since 1967 it has also been produced in clandestine laboratories, frequently in dangerously contaminated forms. The prevailing patterns of street-level abuse are by oral ingestion of tablets or capsules containing the drug in powder form both alone and in combination with other drugs, and by smoking the drug after it has been sprinkled on parsley, marihuana, or some form of tobacco. It is sometimes sold to unsuspecting consumers as LSD, THC, or mescaline. Reported experiences under the influence of phencyclidine are mainly nondescript or unpleasant. In low doses the experience usually proceeds in three successive stages: changes in body image, sometimes accompanied by feelings of depersonalization; perceptual distortions, infrequently evidenced as visual or auditory hallucinations; and feelings of apathy or estrangement. The experience often includes drowsiness, inability to verbalize and feelings of emptiness or "nothingness." Reports of difficulty in thinking, poor concentration, and preoccupation with death are common. Many users have reacted to its use with an acute psychotic episode. Common signs of phencyclidine use include flushing and profuse sweating. Analgesia, involuntary eye movements, muscular incoordination, double vision, dizziness, nausea, and vomiting may also be present.

Chapter 11

DEALING WITH THE DRUG OVERDOSE

WHEN in doubt, scream and shout. In trying to help a person who has taken an overdose of a drug, keep in mind that there is no room for heroics, and don't hesitate to call for assistance. Summon help as fast as you can, since the treatment of a person who has overdosed can represent a life and death situation.

This advice was given by Dr. Sidney Schnoll in a lecture series on the Pharmacology of Substance Abuse sponsored by the Philadelphia Coordinating Office for Drug and Alcohol Abuse Programs (CODAAP).

There is just no telling when you might be confronted with a case of someone suffering from a drug overdose. If you are a parent, it might be your own child or your child's best friend. If you are a teenager, it could be a brother or sister, another relative, or a friend. If you are a teacher, there is always the possibility that a student in one of your classes may collapse from an overdose of drugs. Usually, emergencies of this kind occur when you least expect them. In any event, it makes good sense to know what to do if a drug overdose case happens, and it's just as important to know what *not* to do.

In helping the individual who has overdosed, Dr. Schnoll pointed out, you will doubtless be experiencing great trauma and a drain upon your energy, which can affect how well you react. Don't attempt to handle the emergency by yourself if it can possibly be avoided. Of course, if you are all alone and know that help could be a long time in arriving, do your best to deal with the situation. Collect your thoughts before you do anything.

Remember, if you remain as calm as possible, you will be better able to help the victim. As soon as possible, the individual should be taken to the nearest hospital or other medical facility.

In certain states, the law requires that any hospital receiving state aid must treat drug and alcohol overdose cases. Once a drug is in a person's body, regardless of the route it took to get there, the person taking the drug can no longer be arrested for possession. The law is intentionally designed in this way so that an individual who has taken too much of a drug will seek proper treatment without fear of being "busted." Some type of "Good Samaritan Law" is on the books in most places so that the first aider cannot be held liable for rendering life-saving efforts if done in good faith and without "willful or gross negligence." The immunity is most effective legally if the rescuer has completed and holds current certification in a course of instruction covering basic cardiac life support under Red Cross or American Heart Association standards. The procedures learned in such courses may save the life of a person who has overdosed.

These methods can be used in the treatment of overdose and withdrawal for many drugs including narcotics, sedatives, or stimulants. If you find yourself involved as a first aider, however, don't try to figure out exactly what drug was taken. Even trained medical personnel usually can't do this. Your main concern is to follow the ABCs of basic life support: maintain the victim's *A*irway, *B*reathing and *C*irculation.

Airway

It's very important to make sure that the victim has an adequate airway so that breathing may be possible. People in an overdose situation often vomit or "swallow" their tongues. (In the unconscious victim, the tongue falls against the back of the throat and prevents an adequate airway.) Conscious victims in an upright or sitting position may be choking from the vomitus or other foreign object lodged in the throat. The obstruction must first be relieved to obtain an adequate airway. If the victim is coughing or wheezing heavily, encourage him to cough out the substance; continue, however, to monitor the victim by asking if he can speak. If the airway becomes fully obstructed, the victim will probably clutch his throat and be unable to utter any sound. At this point, tell the victim you will help, then proceed by standing behind the victim and bend him forward at the waist. With one hand support his chest; with the other, give four quick back blows with the heel of the hand high on the back between the shoulder blades with a force intended to dislodge the object. If not relieved, follow immediately with four abdominal thrusts by reaching with your arms around the victim's body, then make a fist and place it thumbside against the choker's abdomen, just slightly above the navel and below the rib cage. Grab your fist with the other hand and press quickly and forcefully into the abdomen with four quick upward and inward thrusts. This combination of four back blows and four abdominal thrusts should be repeated as often as necessary until the obstruction is relieved.

If the victim collapses unconscious, support his fall, turn him over on his back, kneel beside him, and attempt to breathe for him (see breathing procedure described later). If unsuccessful, call for help, then perform the combination of four back blows and abdominal thrusts. First, logroll the victim toward you, give the back blows, turn the victim on his back again, then maneuver your body on an angle to enable you to place one hand on top of the other. putting the heel of your bottom hand on the abdomen as described above, giving the four upward and inward thrusts. If the object is visible, try to sweep it out with your finger(s). The abdominal pressure should be applied within reason depending upon the individual victim. If the victim is a small youth, use less pressure. If the person is of adult size, apply greater pressure. Repeat the sequence starting with an attempt to breathe for the victim each time (followed by the back blows and abdominal thrusts) until successful in dislodging the object, or until help arrives. If successful, then proceed to the *B*reathing step.

You may encounter a person who has taken too much of a drug and who will have already collapsed and be unconscious. Try to wake up the person by shaking him and shouting, "Are you OK?" If the person wakes up or shows a response, then simply monitor the victim and try to assess if you require other help.

What should be done in a case where the victim shows no response? Let's say that you have called for help and several people rush to the scene eager to help in any way possible. Dispatch someone to call the rescue squad or community ambulance or, if appropriate and expeditious, a doctor. In most places the police or fire department paramedics are quick to respond to an emergency call and are well trained to deal with the situation. The emergency number 911 is used in quite a few communities. The person who has made the call should watch for the emergency crew and guide them to the stricken individual. Others who come to the scene should help to deal with the situation until the rescue squad or other assistance arrives. One person, usually the one with the best qualifications in first aid, should take command so that a consistent plan of action is followed and quibbling over what should be done next is avoided. We'll assume that you are the best qualified person on the scene.

Sometimes the airway can be opened simply by lifting up the neck of the victim with one hand (the hand closest to the feet of the victim) while tipping his forehead down with the upper hand. Once the airway is open, place your ear close to the victim's mouth and nose to listen for sounds of breathing. At the same time, look at his chest. You should be able to feel his breath on your cheek and see if his chest is moving. If none of these signs are present, he is not breathing. If opening the airway does not cause the victim to begin breathing, you must provide rescue breathing.

Breathing

The best way to furnish rescue breathing is by using the mouth-to-mouth technique. Take your hand that is on the victim's forehead and turn it so that you can pinch the victim's nostrils shut while keeping the heel of your hand in place to keep the head back. Your other hand should remain under the victim's neck, lifting it up. Next, take a deep breath. Open your mouth widely. Place it over the victim's mouth to provide an airtight seal and blow into the victim's mouth until you see his chest rise. Remove your mouth from the victim. Turn your face toward his chest while listening for the air to escape as he exhales, and look for a falling movement of the chest. If you hear exhalation and see the chest fall, you are performing mouth-to-mouth resuscitation properly. A rate of about 12 breaths a minute (once every five seconds) should be used with an adult or older youth.

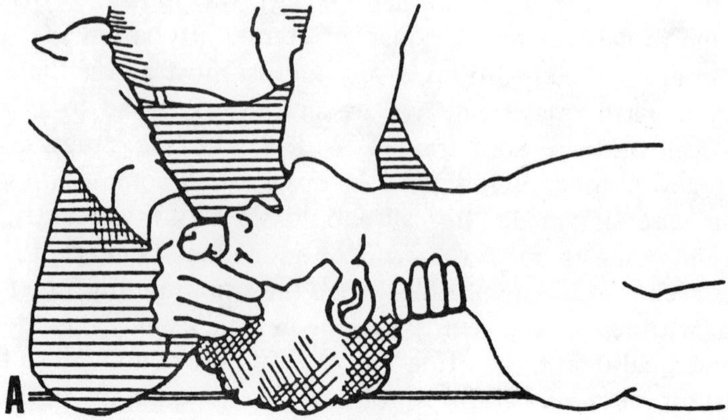

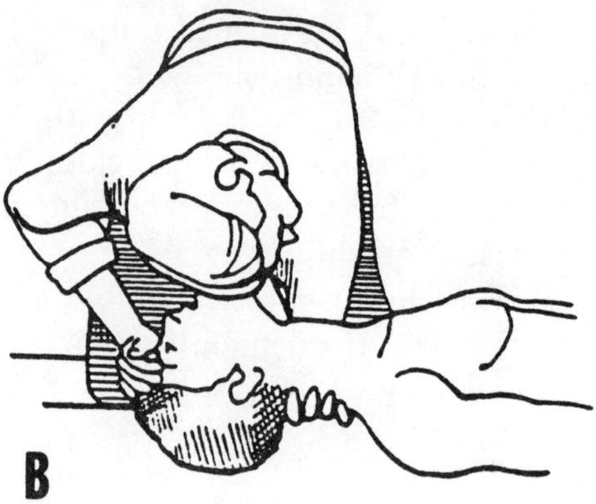

Figure 20. (A) Airway; (B) check breathing.

When you find a victim is not breathing, initially give four quick, full breaths in rapid succession using the mouth-to-mouth method. After given four quick breaths, locate the carotid pulse to see if his heart is beating. Cardiac arrest can be recognized by absent breathing and an absent pulse in the carotid artery in the neck. To find the carotid artery, take your hand that is under the victim's neck and with the index and middle fingers locate the voice box ("Adam's Apple"). Slide the tips of your index and middle fingers along the victim's neck toward you into the groove and "trap" the artery against the neck muscle. Compress this area gently to feel for the pulse in the person's neck for up to 10 sec-

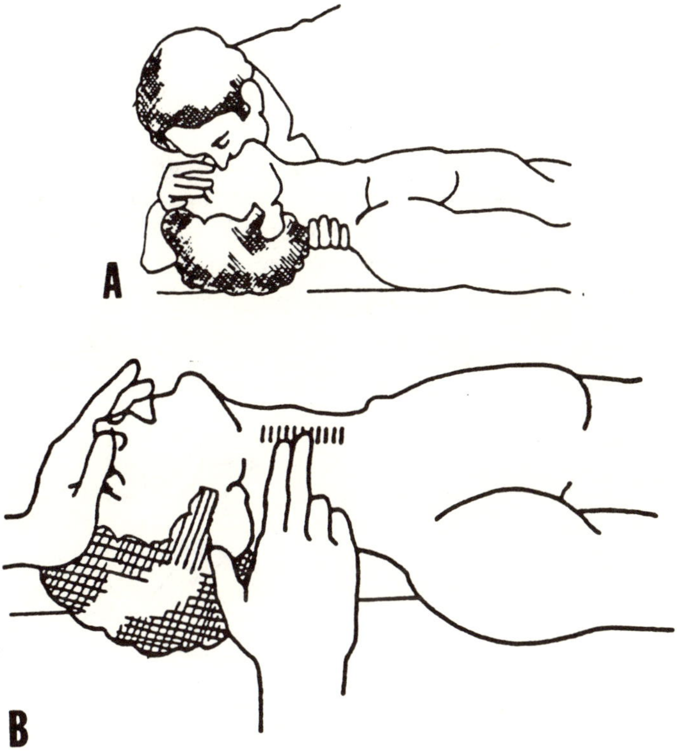

Figure 21. (A) Breathing; (B) check pulse.

onds. If you cannot feel the pulse, you must assume the victim is in cardiac arrest, and you must furnish artificial circulation in addition to rescue breathing. At this point you should have someone call for the emergency medical service response system in that particular area.

Cardiac Compression (Circulation)

Artificial circulation is provided by external cardiac compression. In effect, when you apply rhythmic pressure on the lower half of the victim's sternum, you are forcing his heart to pump blood. To perform external cardiac compression properly, as you are kneeling at the victim's side near his chest, locate – with the middle and index finger of the hand closest to the victim's feet – the notch where the rib cage meets (at the bottom of the sternum or breast bone). Keeping those landmark fingers in place for the moment, place the heel of the other hand next to the index finger of the lower hand. This places the heel of that hand directly over the lower half of the sternum. Then place your lower (landmark) hand on top of the one that is in position. Be sure to keep your fingers off the chest wall. You may find it easier to do this if you interlock your fingers. Proper compressions over this area of the sternum will effect sufficient cardiac output by squeezing the heart between the sternum and the spine.

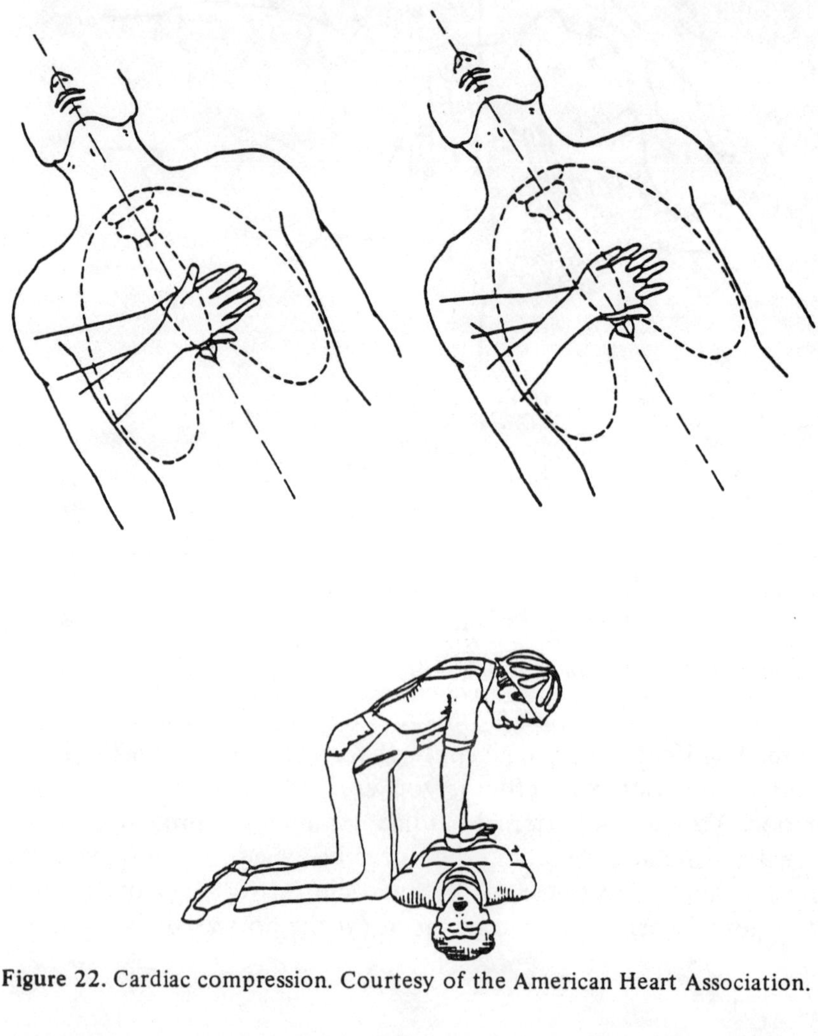

Figure 22. Cardiac compression. Courtesy of the American Heart Association.

Bring your shoulders in a line directly over the victim's sternum as you compress downward, keeping your elbows rigid and arms straight. Depress the sternum about 1½ to 2 inches for an adult-sized victim. Relaxation must follow compression immediately and be of equal time. Remember, do not remove your hands from the victim's sternum while allowing the chest to return to its normal position between compressions, but relieve the pressure on the upstroke.

If you are the only rescuer, you must provide both rescue breathing and cardiac compression, achieving 60 compressions per minute. The proper ratio is 15 chest compressions to 2 quick breaths. Remember, initially you had given *four* quick breaths before checking the pulse. To achieve the 60 per minute compressions, you must compress at the *rate* of 80 times per minute, a little faster than once each second, when you are working alone, since you will lose compressions when you take time to interpose the breaths.

When there is another rescuer to help you, position yourselves on opposite sides of the victim. One of you should be responsible for interposing a breath after every fifth chest compression (on the fifth *upstroke*). The other rescuer who compresses the chest can use a rate of 60 compressions per minute, since no time will be lost for interposing the breaths. Remember, for a single rescuer, the ratio is 15:2 with compressions given at the rate of 80 times per minute. For two rescuers, the ratio of compressions to breath is 5:1 with compressions given at the rate of 60 times per minute.

If a person on drugs goes into a convulsive seizure, the best treatment is to do nothing, other than to prevent the victim from injuring himself. Seizures are usually self-limiting and will stop after a few minutes. After the seizure, the individual will probably want to sleep. Let him sleep or rest, but be sure he is breathing (maintain the airway). Remember, by this time you should have called for the emergency medical services response system in your area.

When a person goes into a seizure, catch him before he falls, if possible, and lower him to a couch or bed or to the floor. A fall against a chair, a cabinet or on the hard wooden floor can be more damaging than the convulsion itself. Don't feel that you must thrust some object such as a pencil or a tongue depresser into the person's mouth to prevent the tongue from being bitten or sucked backward into the throat. Unless the insertion of the object can be done quite easily, don't attempt it. Simply try to keep the head tipped backward to maintain the airway. Using force can cause more harm than good. If you do place an object in the victim's mouth, it is a good idea to wrap it in a small piece of cloth such as a handkerchief before inserting it. The person who has had a seizure should be seen by a doctor as soon as possible.

A very severe type of convulsion is one known as status epilepticus. In this disorder, convulsions are more continuous, and the person does not wake up between episodes. This is a critical situation, and the patient should be gotten to a hospital at once. (Again, the emergency medical services system should have been summoned early in the episode).

If an individual who is withdrawing from a drug is violent or frightened, don't put yourself in the position where you could be injured. If the person grows violent or threatening, simply keep out of the way and call the police. If the individual has a weapon, keep as far from harm's way as possible. Call the police for help.

If the drug user is paranoid, don't approach him from the back. Face him, keep your hands in full view, and walk slowly toward him, if you feel it is the kind of situation you can handle. LSD presents a special situation in which the user may be paranoid or fearful. He may feel that he has lost touch with reality. Try to make gentle physical and verbal contact and attempt to talk him back to reality.

Before leaving our discussion of dealing with emergencies, there are a couple of additional points to be made about victims of choking accidents. Most people don't realize this, but choking on food is the sixth leading cause of accidental death in the United States. Annually more people die by choking than are killed by poisonous snake bites, lightning or electric shock, firearms, or aircraft accidents.

The choking victim becomes quiet. If his airway is fully obstructed, he can't speak, and a terrifying look of alarm usually spreads across his face. He will often clutch tightly at his throat or chest and, if seated, may attempt to rise from his seat. If he is standing, he may even start to run about wildly. If unaided, within just a matter of seconds, the victim will collapse, lose consciousness, and turn blue. He has about four minutes before he will begin to suffer permanent brain damage from lack of oxygen. In less than four more minutes, the victim may die of asphyxiation.

Substance abusers are more likely to be victims of a choking episode than the average person. An individual under the influence may choke while trying to eat or may vomit and choke in the process. Follow the choking sequence as previously described. Whether the back-blows or abdominal thrusts (Heimlich maneuver) are attempted first is of no consequence. It is recommended, however, that the *combination* of the procedures be used.

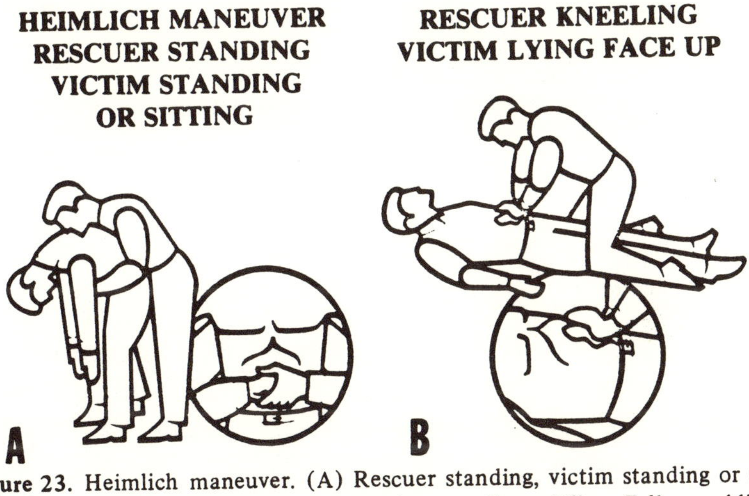

Figure 23. Heimlich maneuver. (A) Rescuer standing, victim standing or sitting. (B) Rescuer kneeling, victim lying face up. From *Pillow Talk*, a publication of Frankford Hospital, Philadelphia, Pennsylvania.

In summary, remember, don't try to be a hero in dealing with an OD, drug withdrawal, or other emergency. Play it safe, get help, know how to give first aid, and follow the other simple steps that have been outlined. Never try home treatments to help the drug abuser such as ice packs and milk injections, since they can boomerang and be dangerous to the individual. There is just no substitute for quickly applying the correct first aid measures and then obtaining proper medical attention as promptly as possible.

It is important to realize that the procedures described above are merely descriptive and informative. They are not intended to be sufficient for the reader to perform these life-saving techniques with proficiency. Only a formal course of instruction will accomplish this. You are urged to register for cardipulmonary resuscitation (CPR) training in basic cardiac life support with your local chapter of the American Heart Association or American Red Cross.

Chapter 12

WHERE TO TURN FOR HELP – RESOURCES IN YOUR COMMUNITY

HAVE your ever wondered how many agencies dealing with drugs, alcohol, and smoking exist in your community? There are probably more such organizations than you realize, because they often have names that do not clearly identify them as organizations that furnish services to people with drug and alcohol problems. The agencies are often known by such names as ACT (Achievement Through Counseling), DRC (Diagnostic and Rehabilitation Center), PATH (People Acting to Help), and RUSH (Racine Underground Safe House). To workers in the drug and alcohol field, the agencies are usually referred to by their acronyms such as ACT, DRC, PATH and RUSH.

The organizations may be known as Environmental Health Centers and carry out programs in particular neighborhoods. Or they may be part of governmental structures such as a Health Department or a Mental Health and Mental Retardation Office and have a citywide program. In some communities, there is a coordinating agency that publishes a directory of all aclohol and drug agencies, making it easier to get in touch with them. In your community, whether it is large or small, there is probably a variety of help for people with drug and alcohol problems. Of course, the larger the community, the more likely it is that there are a number of resources.

The trend today is to include drug and alcohol programs as an important part of public health and place them in health departments, both state and local. In Philadelphia, for example, the drug and alcohol unit is a component of the Philadelphia Department of Public Health. In that city, there are more than 50 agencies having drug and alcohol activities, which operate in about 80 different locations. Included among these agencies are those which emphasize prevention, others that stress early intervention programs and treatment including methadone maintenance, and still others whose main function is rehabilitation. Certain of the agencies concentrate on drug problems, others are oriented toward alcohol abuse and alcoholism, and still others have both drug and alcohol programs in their activities. Philadelphia also has an interagency council on smoking and health, which compiles information about smoking cessation clinics so that people who want to quit smoking can be quickly referred for help. The council also furnishes the general public with information about the harmful effects of smoking not only upon the smoker but also upon the nonsmoker. It also conducts surveys of smoking policies and regulations in government and business.

The Philadelphia Drug and Alcohol System developed over many years with the first agencies in the field originating as separate programs. There were few efforts in the early years to determine whether functions of these agencies complemented one another or overlapped in the same neighborhoods. In the early 1950s, a Division of Mental Health was established in the Health Department. One of the early efforts of this unit was to organize a program on alcohol and drugs. As one segment of the program, an inpatient treatment center of 13 beds was set up for women alcoholics at Philadelphia General Hospital. Other programs included the sponsorship of meetings on drugs and alcohol for school personnel and courses for the Health Department staff.

Using the Drug and Alcohol Unit in Mental Health as a nucleus, the city administration in 1972 organized the Coordinating Office for Drug and Alcohol Abuse Programs (CODAAP) to coordinate the work of agencies functioning at that time in the drug and alcohol field. The aim of the newly founded office was to provide for the city's substance abusers the best possible system of coordinated services. The launching of the new office also showed that the city administration placed a high priority on programs in drugs and alcohol.

At the same time that CODAAP was formed, a Commission on Drugs and Alcohol was established in the city as part of a state requirement for local programs. Known as the Mayor's Executive Commission on Drugs and Alcohol, the body was given the authority for developing an annual Drug and Alcohol Plan. It also was assigned to serve as an advisory body to the director of CODAAP.

Through the efforts of the Mayor's Commission and CODAAP, a well-designed system of drug and alcohol agencies was developed, and each year an annual plan is developed and put into effect. In its role as a coordinating office, CODAAP helps agencies in funding their programs, monitors the programs, and assists in organizing training courses and workshops. CODAAP, which is a major unit in the Health Department, contracts with groups working in the schools to carry out prevention projects.

The problem of drugs, alcohol and smoking in Philadelphia encompasses 12,000 to 15,000 heroin addicts, 30,000 to 50,000 abusers of other drugs, and more than 400,000 adult smokers, about one-third of the adult population. The effects of drugs, alcohol, and smoking are felt by the city's entire population of 1.7 million.

There are hundreds of drug and alcohol programs throughout the nation, and a few of these are described in the remainder of this chapter.

In southwestern Pennsylvania, the Allegheny County Drug and Alcohol Program aims to reduce substance abuse by offering treatment and rehabilitation services. Group and individual counseling is available to drug abusers as well as to their families. The program also strives to help the public, especially youth, not to become alcohol abusers by promoting healthful alternatives to drug use.

To detoxify persons addicted to alcohol and other drugs, residential hospital programs are furnished. Other residential programs located in facilities other than hospitals foster social and personal development in preparing patients to return to the community. Vocational rehabilitation activities help the recovering substance abuser improve chances of finding and keeping employment.

The Driving While Intoxicated Program (DWI) is based on the

belief that prevention through education, self-awareness, and, if needed, treatment is more effective than punishment in reducing death and injuries caused by drunken drivers on the highways. Community prevention and education awareness programs educate the public about the dangers of substance abuse. These programs also promote a better understanding of the problems of abusers and ex-abusers who need rehabilitation.

To insure that all residents have convenient access to help, the county is divided into 11 districts, known as catchment areas. In each catchment area, there is an agency known as a base service unit, which gives information and diagnostic services as well as certain kinds of treatment. Persons needing help can contact the base service unit in their area. Trained professional workers are on hand to determine the person's needs and in cooperation with him or her arrange for services including treatment.

These services are furnished through the base service unit program or through one of a number of additional private agencies that have contracts with the county for more specialized services. In addition, the county operates a 24-hour emergency telephone program.

A representative drug and alcohol program on the West Coast is conducted in Seattle. In that city, the local Drug Abuse Program and the Division of Alcohol Services in the Department of Health were combined as the result of a study carried out by the King County Council in 1980. The combined organization is now known as the Division of Alcohol and Substance Abuse Services of the City Health Department. The responsibility for supervision of policy development for drug and alcohol abuse was given to the King County Alcohol and Substance Abuse Administrative Board.

Contracts have been arranged with six community alcohol centers that have such programs as those encompassing diagnostic and treatment plans, an alcohol information school, an alcohol education program, an outpatient treatment activity, a graduate program, and a spouse and family awareness group. A recent change has been the expansion of services to the community alcohol centers to include information, assessment, and outpatient treatment services to drug abusing clients.

In Los Angeles, the Drug Abuse Program Office (DAPO) is

located in the Department of Health Services. DAPO is responsible for the provision and coordination of drug abuse treatment, prevention and education, and support services for the residents of Los Angeles County.

The Public Information and Referral Unit of DAPO manages and coordinates residential detoxification services as well as a number of public information and education activities. The unit furnishes literature, films, and other aids and also organizes programs for parents, schools, community groups, and law enforcement agencies. In addition the unit makes referrals for prevention or treatment services.

A function of the Courts and Jails Service Unit is to provide a comprehensive advocacy service for drug dependent inmates who are imprisoned in county jails. The unit also works closely with the County Sheriff's Department in carrying out drug abuse awareness classes. Youths, parents, teachers, county correctional staff and members of school systems are given information on drug abuse and support services by the Outreach Services Unit. Among the functions of this unit are the First Offender Project consisting of presentations on positive life-style in probation camps and drug prevention and education programs for probation camps, schools, and neighborhood agencies.

Among other units is the Prevention and Education Unit, which has as its main job the management of DAPO's 20 prevention contracts. The unit also develops a countywide prevention plan to meet the needs of certain target populations. Services given by both the schools and the community are used in this effort.

Among agencies that publish guidebooks on programs in their area is the Omaha-Douglas County Health Department, which has its headquarters in Omaha. The department distributes a directory of agencies operating in the alcohol field. Among them are Al-Anon, Alcoholics Anonymous, American Indians Center Alcoholism Program, Methodist Midtown Creighton Prep, Operation Bridge, and Saint Monica's. Although a directory of drug agencies is not currently published, there are a number of programs at work in the drug field. Among these are the Equilibrium Medical Clinic, Operation Bridge, Pride of Omaha, Eastern Nebraska Community Office of Mental Health, and Immanuel Community Mental Health Program.

The Milwaukee Council on Drug Abuse publishes an Information and Referral Handbook covering a wide range of health services. Drug and Alcohol programs are included in the directory, and the listing of drug and substance abuse facilities has among others Cornerstone Community Center, De Paul Bellevue Extended Care, Families Anonymous, Fourth Street Program, Genesis, Midtown Clinic, Kettle Moraine Hospital, Milwaukee Council on Drug Abuse, Racine Underground Safe House, Underground Switchboard, and Narcotics Anonymous.

Alcohol Services listed include Community Resources, Inc.; Comprehensive Care, Inc.; De Paul Rehabilitation Hospital; Dewey Center Dodge County Unified Services; Downtown Medical Health Service; Families Anonymous; Women and Alcohol Project; Women Reaching Women; and Silver Springs Neighborhood Center.

The Resource Guide published by the Philadelphia Coordinating Office for Drug and Alcohol Abuse Programs (CODAAP) lists drug and alcohol provider agency services under a number of different headings including Special Services for Women. Among agencies listed in the directory, which comprises programs in much of the Philadelphia Metropolitan Area, are the Bridge; Congreso do Latinos Unidos; CORA Services; Family Center Program; Gaundenzia Outreach Community Center; Genesis II; HELP, Inc. Drug Program; Horizon House; Lower Kensington Environmental Center; Aurora House; Elizabeth Blackwell Health Center for Women; Women for Sobriety; and Teen Challenge Girls Home.

An example of a directory put out at the state level is the Maryland Directory of Treatment Resources. The publication is updated annually to satisfy the many requests for information on state and local treatment facilities. Data for the directory were extracted from the National Drug and Alcoholism Treatment Utilization Survey conducted in 1979.

The directory points out that if alcohol treatment services have not been started in your community, you can obtain help from a variety of individuals and organizations. The list of individuals who can furnish assistance includes clergymen, family doctors, public health nurses, and social workers. Among organizations that can give help are Alcoholics Anonymous, Al-Anon, alcoholism information and referral centers, community mental health centers, Veterans Administration or general hospitals, health services, welfare or family services, many employers and labor unions, and local office of the National Council on Alcoholism.

In the directory, treatment facilities are listed alphabetically whenever possible and grouped first by city (when county information is unavailable), then by county.

As these guidebooks indicate, most communities have organized drug and alcohol programs. To find out just what your community offers, there are several institutions you can call upon for information, which will gladly give help. These include your local health department, always an excellent source of information on health matters, the Health and Welfare Agency in your area, the local Health Systems Agency (HSA), the state or county medical or osteopathic societies, the community nursing services, and the Chamber of Commerce. Hospitals are also good sources of information about drug and alcohol programs, since the hospital emergency rooms are called upon to treat people who overdose, and the hospitals frequently refer patients back to such agencies for additional treatment and rehabilitation. Questions about smoking and health programs can also be directed to the agencies we have just listed.

Once you have obtained the details about the system in your community, a telephone call or visit to the particular organization that bests suits your needs will furnish all the information required. We have described several communities that have guidebooks giving complete information about the type of program, hours of operation, fees, program descriptions, and, of course, addresses, telephone numbers, and names of contact persons. Such guide books are usually available without charge through the local groups that coordinate the neighborhood drug and alcohol programs. Copies of the directors are also likely to be found in the resource sections of public libraries.

There are also numerous agencies at the state and national levels. The listing of single state agencies is found at the end of this chapter. Nationwide, there are such agencies as the National Institute on Drug Abuse (NIDA), the National Institute on Alcohol Abuse and Alcoholism (NIAAA), and the National Council on

Alcoholism (NCA). In addition to publishing a variety of publications, these organizations conduct special programs and carry out research studies.

Among national organizatons in the drug, alcohol and smoking fields are the following:

Smoking Cessation

Technical Information Center
Office on Smoking and Health, 5600 Fishers Lane, Room 1-16
Rockville, Maryland 20850

The Office of Cancer Communications, National Cancer Institute
Room 10A18, Bldg. 31, National Institutes of Health
Bethesda, Maryland 20014

The American Lung Association, 1740 Broadway
New York, New York 10019 (or local chapter)

The American Heart Association, 7320 Greenville Avenue
Dallas, Texas 75331 (or local chapter)

Alcohol and Drug Abuse Reduction

National Clearinghouse for Drug Abuse Information
National Institute on Drug Abuse
P.O. Box 1701, Washington, D.C. 20013

National Clearinghouse for Alcohol Information
National Institute for Alcohol Abuse and Alcoholism
P.O. Box 2345, Rockville, Maryland 20850

National Clearinghouse for Mental Health Information
National Institute of Mental Health
U.S. Department of Health and Human Services
5600 Fishers Lane, Room 1-16, Rockville, Maryland 20857

The National Council on Alcoholism, 733 Third Avenue
New York, New York 10017

Alcoholics Anonymous, Public Information Department
468 Park Avenue, New York New York 10016

Single State Agencies

ALABAMA
Drug Abuse Program Section
Division of Alcoholism and Drug Abuse
Department of Mental Health
135 S. Union
Montgomery, Alabama 36130

ALASKA
Office of Drug Abuse
Dept. of Health & Social Services
Pouch H-05F
Juneau, Alaska 99811

ARIZONA
Drug Abuse Programs
Division of Behavioral Health Services
Department of Health Services
2500 East Van Buren
Phoenix, Arizona 85008

ARKANSAS
Office of Drug and Alcohol Abuse Prevention
Dept. of Social & Rehab. Services
1515 Building
1515 West 7th
Little Rock, Arkansas 72203

CALIFORNIA
California Department of Alcohol and Drug Abuse
111 Capital Mall
Sacramento, California 95814

COLORADO
Alcohol & Drug Abuse Division
Department of Health
4210 East 11th Avenue
Denver, Colorado 80220

CONNECTICUT
Connecticut Alcohol and Drug Council
Department of Mental Health
90 Washington Street
Hartford, Connecticut 06115

DELAWARE
Bureau of Substance Abuse
1901 N. Dupont Highway
New Castle, Delaware 19720

FLORIDA
Bureau of Drug Abuse Prevention
Division of Mental Health
Dept. of Health & Rehab. Services
1317 Winewood Blvd.
Tallahassee, Florida 32301

GEORGIA
Alcohol and Drug Abuse Section
Div. of Mental Health & Retardation
Department of Human Resources
618 Ponce De Leon Avenue, N.E.
Atlanta, Georgia 30308

HAWAII
Alcohol and Drug Abuse Branch
Department of Health
1270 Queen Emma Street, Room 404
Honolulu, Hawaii 96813

IDAHO
Bureau of Substance Abuse
Division of Community Rehabilitation
Department of Health and Welfare
700 West State Street
Boise, Idaho 83720

ILLINOIS
Dangerous Drugs Commission
300 North State Street, 15th Floor
Chicago, Illinois 60610

INDIANA
Division of Addiction Services
Department of Mental Health
5 Indiana Square
Indianapolis, Indiana 46204

IOWA
Iowa Drug Abuse Authority
505 5th Avenue
Des Moines, Iowa 50319

KANSAS
Drug Abuse Unit
Dept. of Social and Rehab. Services
Biddle Bldg.
2700 W. 6th Street
Topeka, Kansas 66608

KENTUCKY
Alcohol and Drug Abuse Branch
Division for Prevention Services
Bureau of Health Services
Department of Human Resources
275 East Main Street
Frankfort, Kentucky 40601

LOUISIANA
Bureau of Substance Abuse
Division of Hospitals
Louisiana Health and Human
Resource Administration
200 Lafayette Street
Baton Rouge, Louisiana 70804

MAINE
Office of Alcoholism and Drug
Abuse Prevention
Bureau of Rehabilitation
32 Winthrop Street
Augusta, Maine 04330

MARYLAND
Drug Abuse Administration
Dept. of Health & Mental Hygiene
Herbert O'Conor Office Building
201 W. Preston Street
Baltimore, Maryland 21201

MASSACHUSETTS
Division of Drug Rehabilitation
Department of Mental Health
160 N. Washington Street
Boston, Massachusetts 02114

MICHIGAN
Office of Substance Abuse Services
3500 North Logan Street
P.O. Box 30035
Lansing, Michigan 48909

MINNESOTA
Drug and Alcohol Authority
Chemical Dependency Division
Dept. of Public Welfare
658 North Cedar Street
St. Paul, Minnesota 55155

MISSISSIPPI
Division of Drug Misuse
Department of Mental Health
619 Lee State Office Building
Jackson, Mississippi 39201

MISSOURI
Division of Alcoholism & Drug
Abuse
Department of Mental Health
2002 Missouri Blvd.
Jefferson City, Missouri 65101

MONTANA
Addictive Diseases Division
Department of Institutions
1539 11th Avenue
Helena, Montana 59601

NEBRASKA
Nebraska Commission on Drugs
P.O. Box 94726
State Capitol Building

Lincoln, Nebraska 68509

NEVADA
Bureau of Alcohol & Drug Abuse
Rehabilitation Division
Department of Human Resources
505 East King Street
Carson City, Nevada 89710

NEW HAMPSHIRE
Office of Drug Abuse Prevention
3 Capital Street, Room 405
Concord, New Hampshire 03301

NEW JERSEY
Division of Narcotic and Drug
Abuse Control
Department of Health
129 East Hanover Street
Trenton, New Jersey 08625

NEW MEXICO
Drug Abuse Agency
Department of Hospitals &
Institutions
P.O. Box 968
Santa Fe, New Mexico 87503

NEW YORK
Office of Drug Abuse Services
Executive Park South
Albany, New York 12203

NORTH CAROLINA
North Carolina Drug Commission
325 N. Salisbury Street
Raleigh, North Carolina 27611

NORTH DAKOTA
Division of Alcoholism and Drug
Abuse
Department of Health
909 Basin Avenue
Bismark, North Dakota 58505

OHIO
Ohio Bureau of Drug Abuse
Division of Mental Health
Department of Mental Health and
Mental Retardation
65 S. Front Street, Room 211
Columbus, Ohio 43215

OKLAHOMA
Division of Drug Abuse Services
Department of Mental Health
P.O. Box 53277, Capitol Station
Oklahoma City, Oklahoma 73105

OREGON
Program for Alcohol and Drug
Problems
Mental Health Division
Department of Human Resources
2575 Bittern Street, N.E.
Salem, Oregon 97310

PENNSYLVANIA
Office of Drug and Alcohol
Programs
Department of Health
P.O. Box 90
Harrisburg, Pa. 17120

RHODE ISLAND
Rhode Island Drug Abuse
Program
Department of Mental Health and
Retardation and Hospitals
303 General Hospital
Rhode Island Medical Center
Cranston, Rhode Island 02920

SOUTH CAROLINA
South Carolina Commission on
Alcohol and Drug Abuse
3700 Forest Drive
P.O. Box 4616
Columbus, South Carolina 29240

SOUTH DAKOTA
Division of Drugs and Substance Control
Department of Health
Joe Foss Building
Pierre, South Dakota 57501

TENNESSEE
Alcohol and Drug Abuse Section
Department of Mental Health
501 Union Street, 4th Floor
Nashville, Tennessee 37219

TEXAS
Drug Abuse Division
Department of Community Affairs
Box 12166, Capitol Station
Austin, Texas 78711

UTAH
Division of Alcoholism and Drugs
150 N. Temple
Salt Lake City, Utah 84110

VERMONT
Alcohol and Drug Abuse Division
Department of Social & Rehab. Services
State Office Building
Montpelier, Vermont 05602

VIRGINIA
Department of Mental Health/ Mental Retardation
Division of Substance Abuse Control
Commonwealth of Virginia
P.O. Box 1797
Richmond, Virginia 23214

WASHINGTON
Office of Drug Abuse Prevention
Community Services Division
DSHS, OB-43E
Olympia, Washington 98504

BIBLIOGRAPHY

1. Alcoholics Anonymous World Services, *A Community Resource for Coping with a National Health Problem,* New York, N.Y., 1975.
2. Alcoholics Anonymous, *This is A.A.*, New York, N.Y., 1977.
3. Aldrich, Michael, *A Brief Legal History of Marijuana,* Do It Now Foundation, Phoenix, Ariz.
4. Allegheny County Drug and Alcohol Abuse Program, *Drug and Alcohol Services,* Pittsburgh, Pa.
5. Allen, William A., Gerhard Angermann, and William A. Fackler, *Learning to Live Without Cigarettes,* Doubleday and Co., Inc., New York, N.Y., 1973.
6. American Automobile Association, *One Drink Can Be Too Many,* Falls Church, Va., 1975.
7. American Cancer Society, *The Decision is Yours,* New York, N.Y., 1978.
8. Blue Cross and Blue Shield, *Alcoholism,* Philadelphia, Pa., 1979.
9. Blue Cross and Blue Shield, *Drug Abuse – Drugs in a Chemical Dependent Society,* Philadelphia, Pa., 1978.
10. Brechter, Edward M., *Licit and Illicit Drugs,* Consumers Union Report, Little, Brown and Co., Boston, Mass., 1972.
11. Bureau of Traffic Safey, *Drugged Drivers – What Can a Pill Do to Your Driving Reactions?* Harrisburg, Pa.
12. Channing L. Bete Company, Inc., *About Drug Abuse,* South Deerfield, Ma., 1981.
13. Channing L. Bete Company, Inc., *Drugs and You,* South Deerfield, Ma., 1981.
14. Channing L. Bete Company, Inc., *What Every Teenager Should Know About Alcohol,* South Deerfield, Ma., 1980.
15. Coordinating Office for Drug and Alcohol Abuse Programs, Launch New Alcohol Highway Safety Program, *CODAAP REPORT,* Philadelphia, Pa., July/August, 1982.
16. Coordinating Office for Drug and Alcohol Abuse Programs, New Hazard for Marijuana Smokers, *CODAAP REPORT,* Philadelphia, Pa., March/April, 1982.
17. Coordinating Office for Drug and Alcohol Abuse Programs, Prevention is people business, *CODAAP Report,* Philadelphia, Pa., May, 1981.

18. Coordinating Office for Drug and Alcohol Abuse Programs, Proceedings of Lecture Series, *Pharmacology of Substance Abuse,* Philadelphia, Pa., 1976.
19. *Digest of Alcoholism Theory and Application,* Clinical effect of fetal alcohol syndrome, Johnson Institute, Minneapolis, Minnesota, January, 1982.
20. *Digest of Alcoholism Theory and Application,* Family rituals and the transmission of alcoholism. Johnson Institute, Minneapolis, Minn., October, 1981.
21. Do It Now Foundation, *Facts About Your Body's Health, Vitamins and Alcohol and Related Polydrug Abuse,* Phoenix, Ariz., 1974.
22. Do It Now Foundation, *Junk and You,* Phoenix, Ariz., 1976.
23. Drug Enforcement Administration, *The Current Challenge, Southwest Asian Heroin,* Washington, D.C., Summer, 1981.
24. Drug Enforcement Administration, *Summary of Drug Control Activities under the Controlled Substance Act of 1970,* Washington, D.C.
25. Ewing, John A. and Beatrice A. Rouse, *Drinking – Alcohol in American Society, Issues and Current Research,* Nelson-Hall, Chicago, Ill., 1978.
26. *Family Circle,* The deadliest duo, New York, N.Y., September, 16, 1982.
27. Governor's Traffic Safety Council, *How to Deal with Teenage Drinking and Driving,* Harrisburg, Pa.
28. Greater Philadelphia Interagency Council on Smoking and Health, *Legislation Prohibits Smoking in Patient Rooms and Other Areas in Hospitals,* Philadelphia, Pa. 1977.
29. Hopper, C. Edmund and William A. Allen, *Sex Education for Physically Handicapped Youth,* Charles C Thomas, Springfield, Ill., 1980.
30. *How To Keep the Life of the Party Alive,* Harrisburg, Pa.
31. *International Journal of Addictions,* Alcohol abuse in ancient Egypt: The recorded evidence, New York, N.Y., Vol. 16, No. 7, 1981.
32. *International Journal of Addictions,* When drugs come into the picture, love flies out the window: Women addicts love relationships, New York, N.Y., Vol. 16, No. 7, 1981.
33. Josephson, S., Scuba diving hazards: Health counseling, *American Journal of Nursing,* New York, N.Y., August, 1981.
34. King County Division of Alcohol and Substance Abuse Services, *Seattle-King County Community Alcohol Centers Services,* Seattle, Washington, 1981.
35. *Listen Magazine,* Blowing dates up in smoke, Washington, D.C., January, 1981.
36. *Listen Magazine,* Why drugs and sex don't mix, Washington, D.C., January, 1981.
37. Mariken, Gene and Eugene Scheimann, *Alcohol and Alcoholism,* Budlong Press, Chicago, Ill., 1969.
38. Milwaukee Council on Drug Abuse, Inc., *Information and Referral Handbook,* Milwaukee, Wis., 1981.

39. *Narcotics Education,* If you smoke, here's what your doctor may see. Washington, D.C.
40. National Clearinghouse for Alcohol Information, *Think Before You Drink,* Washington, D.C., 1976.
41. National Council on Alcoholism, Delaware Valley Area, Inc., *The Effect of Alcoholism on Children,* Philadelphia, Pa., 1976.
42. National Council on Alcoholism, *Kids and Alcohol,* New York, N.Y.
43. National Council on Alcoholism, *A Teachers Manual for Use with Jackson Junior High,* New York, N.Y.
44. National Highway Traffic Safety Administration, *You, Alcohol and Driving,* Washington, D.C.
45. National Institute on Alcohol Abuse and Alcoholism, *Alcohol and Your Unborn Baby,* Rockville, Md., 1978.
46. National Institute on Alcohol Abuse and Alcoholism, *Play it Smart. Facts for Teenagers about Drinking,* Rockville, Md., 1981.
47. New Book of Knowledge, *Beer and Brewing,* Grolier, Inc., New York, N.Y., 1969.
48. *Newsweek,* Curbing drunk drivers, New York, N.Y., January 25, 1982.
49. *Newsweek,* The war against drunk drivers, New York, N.Y., September 13, 1982.
50. *New York Times,* Research on marijuana finds many risks, some benefits, New York, N.Y., October 9, 1979.
51. Omaha-Douglas County Health Department, *Directory of Alcohol Services,* Omaha, Neb.
52. *Ottawa Citizen,* Smokers wisps do more harm than believed. Ottawa, Canada, July 23, 1982.
53. Pennsylvania Chamber of Commerce, *Alcoholism,* Harrisburg, Pa., 1978.
54. *Philadelphia Bulletin,* Don't count on drugs to help sex performance, Philadelphia, Pa. September 24, 1979.
55. *Philadelphia Daily News,* Kicking the habit, Philadelphia, Pa., June 16, 1982.
56. *Philadelphia Daily News,* Series on drug abuse in professional sports, February-March, 1982.
57. Philadelphia Department of Public Health, *Is Air Pollution Worse for the Smoker?* Air Pollution Control Progress, Philadelphia, Pa., August, 1968.
58. *Philadelphia Inquirer,* Cigarettes: Koop issues strong warning to nonsmokers, Philadelphia, Pa., February 23, 1982.
59. *Philadelphia Inquirer,* Probe: Boat turned too sharply in fatal Bucks Accidents, Philadelphia, Pa., April 2, 1982.
60. *Philadelphia Inquirer,* Stiffer law backed for Drunkenness, Philadelphia, Pa., August 25, 1982.
61. *Philadelphia Inquirer,* Worlds's heroin supplier is also getting hooked, Philadelphia, Pa., August 30, 1982.
62. Proprietary Association, *Drug Abuse and Your Child,* Washington, D.C. 1971.

63. Public Affairs Pamphlet No. 515, *Drugs – Use, Misuse, Abuse, Guidance for Families,* New York, N.Y., 1979.
64. *Reader's Digest,* Do you know what happens when you smoke? Pleasantville, N.Y., July, 1972.
65. Russell, George K., *Marijuana Today,* The Myrin Institute for Adult Education, New York, N.Y., 1978.
66. Schmidt, J.E., *Medical Discoveries – Where and When,* Charles C Thomas, Springfield, Ill. 1959.
67. Smith, Kline and French Laboratories, *Drug Abuse – Escape to Nowhere,* Philadelphia, Pa., 1970.
68. Smith, Kline and French Laboratories, *Drug Abuse – The Empty Life,* Philadelphia, Pa., 1967.
69. *Smoke Signals,* Smoking's strangest disease, American Temperance Society, Washington, D.C., 1967.
70. Special Action Office for Drug Abuse Prevention, *Questions and Answers about Drug Abuse,* Washington, D.C., 1975.
71. *Today's Health,* Warning: Is your sex life going up in smoke? Chicago, Ill. August, 1974.
72. U.S. Department of Health, Education and Welfare, *It Starts with People – Experiences in Drug Abuse Prevention,* Rockville, Md., 1978.
73. U.S. Department of Health and Human Services, *Drug Abuse Prevention for Older Americans,* Washington, D.C., 1978.
74. U.S. Department of Health and Human Services, *Drug Abuse Prevention for your Family,* Rockville, Md., 1980.
75. U.S. Department of Health and Human Services, *Drugs and Driving,* Rockville, Md., 1979.
76. U.S. Department of Health and Human Services, *Here's to your Health,* Rockville, Md., 1981.
77. U.S. Department of Health and Human Services. *Law and Legislative Summaries, States,* Washington, D.C., 1980.
78. U.S. Department of Health and Human Services, *Maryland Directory of Treatment Resources,* Rockville, Md., 1980.
79. U.S. Department of Health and Human Services, *Smoking and Health Bulletin,* Rockville, Md., 1980.
80. U.S. Department of Justice, *Drug Abuse and Misuse,* Washington, D.C., 1979.
81. U.S. Department of Justice, *Drug Enforcement,* Washington, D.C., 1979.
82. U.S. Department of Justice, *Guidelines for Prescribers of Controlled Substances,* Washington, D.C., 1980.
83. U.S. Department of Transportation, *An Activist's Guide for Curbing the Drunk Driver,* Washington, D.C., April, 1977.
84. U.S. Department of Transportation, *Communications Strategies on Alcohol and Highway Safety,* Washington, D.C., 1975.
85. U.S. Department of Transportation, *The Problem Drinker and You,* Washington, D.C., 1974.

86. U.S. Department of Transportation, *You . . . Alcohol and Driving,* Washington, D.C.
87. U.S. Food and Drug Administration, *Drugs and Driving,* Washington, D.C., 1965.
88. *U.S. Journal of Drug and Alcohol Dependence,* Cigarette packages, stronger health warnings considered, Miami, Fla., 1981.
89. *U.S. Journal of Drug and Alcohol Dependence,* Drunk Driving Commission gets rolling, Miami, Fla., June, 1982.
90. *U.S. Journal of Drug and Alcohol Dependence,* Marijuana research should be intensified. Miami, Fla., March, 1981.
91. *U.S. Journal of Drug and Alcohol Dependence,* Tough action sought at federal level, Miami, Fla., March, 1981.
92. Wright, Samson, *Applied Physiology,* Oxford University Press, London, England, 1955.
93. Zubin, Joseph and Alfred M. Freedman, *The Psychopathology of Adolescence,* Grune and Stratton, New York and London, 1970.

INDEX